VIGIL

VIGIL

ALAN SHAPIRO

THE UNIVERSITY

OF CHICAGO PRESS

CHICAGO AND LONDON

Alan Shapiro is professor of English and creative writing at the University of North Carolina at Chapel Hill. He is the author of five books of poetry, including *Mixed Company,* which won the 1996 *Los Angeles Times* award for poetry. His memoir *The Last Happy Occasion* was a finalist for the 1996 National Book Critics Circle award for biography/autobiography.

The University of Chicago Press, Chicago 60637
The University of Chicago Press, Ltd., London
© 1997 by The University of Chicago
All rights reserved. Published 1997
07 06 05 04 03 02 01 00 99 98   1 2 3 4 5

ISBN: 0-226-75034-5

Library of Congress Cataloging-in-Publication Data

Shapiro, Alan, 1952–
     Vigil / Alan Shapiro.
         p.   cm.
     ISBN 0-226-75034-5
     1. Shapiro, Beth—Health.   2. Terminally ill—United States—
Biography.   3. Interracial marriage.   4. Shapiro, Alan, 1952–   —
Biography.   5. Poets, American—20th century—Biography.
6. Jews—United States—Biography.   I. Title.
R726.8.S475S53   1997
362.1'9699449'0092—dc21
     [B]   97-3247
                                                                           CIP

For my mother,

whose vigil was the longest

and most loving

Contents

‘

I want to thank Kathryn Rhett, editor of *Survivor Stories* (Anchor/Doubleday), in which "The Vision" in an earlier form first appeared, and Richard Burgin, editor of *Boulevard,* for publishing "The Summoning."

Arthur Frank, Rafael Campo, and Morris Dickstein made many helpful and sensitive suggestions that greatly improved the book, and to them I want to give my heartfelt thanks. Throughout the difficult process of writing this book, I've been blessed with friends and editors whose judgment, impeccable taste, and astonishing insight kept me honest when I didn't want to be, and whose undiscourageable faith in the book itself kept me going when I otherwise would have quit. My debt to Randolph Petilos and Alan Thomas is unrepayable, as is my debt to Tom Sleigh, David Ferry, Robert Pinsky, Tobias Wolff, John Rosenthal, Jason Sommer, Reginald Gibbons, Cornelia Spelman, Robert von Hallberg, and C. K. Williams. No writer ever had better editors for friends, or better friends for editors.

Finally, I want to thank my wife, Della Pollock, not only for her crucial help with every page I've written, but for all the other sacrifices (too many to number) that she made on my and this book's behalf.

VIGIL

*T*he day before she died I had a vision of my sister. I was lying on the floor beside her bed, my feet up on a chair, the only position that relieved the back pain I'd been having ever since I moved into the hospice with her four weeks earlier. Her half-filled urine bag was level with my head. On my other side my father, nearly blind, had pulled a chair just inches from the television screen so he could watch the O. J. Simpson trial. Or appear at least to watch it, for, as he always would, he fell asleep as soon as he sat down, his head nodding lower and lower till now and again he'd start awake and say, as if to prove he wasn't sleeping and hadn't missed a moment of the court proceedings, "He's gonna walk, I'm tellin' ya, guilty as sin, he's gonna walk. . . ." On the couch beyond him, my mother and brother were leaning forward over the book of crossword puzzles open before them on the ottoman. They'd started the book three weeks ago and now were working on the final puzzle. From time to time, one of them would ask my father or me for help—my father for the sports questions, me for the literary ones.

"Defensive end of the Steel Curtain, begins with 'm,' ends with 'e,' thirteen letters."

"Mean Joe Greene," my Dad would call out dreamily, not even opening his eyes.

"Okay, professor, de Beauvoir's beau, six letters."

"Seven letters," was how I usually responded, whether or not I knew the answer. "Means 'No I don't, couldn't be bothered, get lost,' begins with 'f,' ends with 'f,' two words, first word rhymes with *puck*."

The room had a familial intimacy, spacious yet cozy; the furnishings, the walls, even the painting, propped on a cabinet shelf, of a horse and English rider were tastefully done in soft tones, varieties of beige and brown, designed to make us feel if not at home exactly, then as far from a medical institution as a medical institution could be. If my sister hadn't been there dying, you'd have thought we were a normal family on a normal day, absorbed in ordinary and habitual pleasures, pursuits, preoccupations. What we, in fact, were doing, had been doing now for several weeks, was performing ordinary life, and the better and more convincing the performance, the more estranged we felt from the lives we left behind us when my sister began to die in earnest.

Beth's dying had become a new reality, too all-encompassing to be constantly perceived or felt, yet too heightened in its strangeness to be ever out of mind. It shadowed the most mundane activities we used to do unthinkingly and now could not do without thinking how peculiar it was that we were doing them at all. Day in, day out, sitting beside my sister I would ask my father how the BoSox did last night, did the Yankees win, could Roger Clemens ever come back from his elbow problems, and do the bums really have a chance without him, and while I spoke I'd hear myself speaking, see myself turned to my father, listening as he answered, wondering at our intonations, at our gestures, how our hands waved to emphasize a point, each of us arguing our positions as if nothing in the world were more important. Or afternoons when I'd go out to get our lunch at the local supermarket, as I picked this or that thing off the shelf, or stood waiting while the woman at the deli took her sweet time making the sandwiches I ordered, or as I placed my basket on the checkout counter, answering the bagger that I wanted plastic, please, not paper, and then paid, and lugged my few bags to the car, I'd think how much I must have looked like any other customer on just another day of errands, and not someone whose sister was dying just a mile down the road. I seemed to hover outside my body in the charged atmosphere of Beth's impending death, while my body went on pretending I was who I always was. I lived, we all lived, with a doubled, dreamlike consciousness of what we all were going through, bewildered most by what remained familiar, like anthropologists discovering that the never-before-encountered culture they're observing is their own.

We had fallen abruptly out of life into a virtual existence in which time was measured mostly by my sister's failing body, her moment-to-moment changes in respiration, temperature, intake of food or fluids, by how long it took her urine bag to fill, how often she needed morphine, and in what amounts. The hospice room became a universe in which the terms of life were simultaneously narrowed and intensified. And in keeping with the inherent doubleness of every state of feeling, however much we suffered as we watched my sister die, we didn't merely suffer. There was joy, too, or something like joy, in the suffering itself. Joy in the self-forgetfulness that came with tending Beth, with grieving for her, and in caring so tenderly for each other as we grieved; joy in the dissolution of the opaque privacies of daily life, in the heightened clarity of purpose and desire, in the transparency of understanding we all felt for the first time as a family; joy, in other words, in an intimacy whose very rarity added sadness to the joy.

By "we," I should add, I mean my mother, my father, my brother, and me. That familial intimacy, however, intense as it was, still had to compete for each of us in varying degrees with other claims on our attention. My father, for instance, was intermittently distracted by his various ailments, his Parkinson's syndrome, the fatigue from his insomnia, his general disorientation at being far from home. My brother, an actor, arrived from Pittsburgh at the end of the first week when the show he was doing there had ended. A week later he went to New York for another job and then returned to Houston during the final week. During this time as well his daughter in California had gotten sick. Hepatitis was the initial diagnosis. It turned out not to be, but for several days he was very worried about her, always calling home. Shortly after I arrived in Houston, my wife badly sprained her ankle, generating a flurry of calls to her, to my children. Like my brother, I too felt the need to be in two places at once. Only my mother remained completely focused on Beth throughout the whole ordeal, her attentions unclaimed by any other need or obligation.

My sister's husband, Russ, was a peripheral figure at the hospice. Usually Russ visited only in the early evenings after picking up their daughter, Gabbi, from horseback-riding camp. Tired, hungry, and every bit her seven years of age, Gabbi would grow restless almost immediately, especially once Beth had lost her ability to speak or respond, and Russ would have to take her home. Gabbi, it was clear to all of us, to Beth especially, provided Russ with a reason not to stay too long. That's why he never came without her. Once Beth was moved into the hospice, and her condition worsened, he withdrew—from her, from us, perhaps from the overwhelming sorrow of it all. Beth at times seemed wounded by his absence, and for her sake I was angry with him. At the same time, I knew he had his reasons. He was diagnosed with heart disease around the same time Beth was diagnosed with cancer. I can only imagine what his anxiety and fear on Beth's behalf were doing to his already weakened heart. And then there was his history: his mother's death from cancer (the same cancer that was killing Beth) when he was five, his father's of a heart attack a year later. I knew that Beth's illness had awakened all the devastating traumas of his childhood. I also knew that as a black man married to a white woman he never felt entirely at ease around her family. And his history with us, my father especially, was not a happy one.

For years my father would not accept Russ as his son-in-law. Early in Beth and Russ's relationship, my father refused to let Russ visit on the holidays. He refused to introduce him to his family back in Boston. And when Della and I got married, he threatened to dis-invite his relatives from the wedding if Della and I invited Russ. We did, of course. But Russ decided not to come, not wanting to go anywhere he wasn't welcome. Through it all, while Beth raged at my father's ignorance and selfishness, Russ himself remained imperturbable. From hard experience, he'd long since come to expect nothing else from most white people. He even calmly tried to talk my sister into going to the wedding out of loyalty to me. After Gabbi was born, my father came around enough at least to recognize Russ as his daughter's husband, if not to love him as he loved my brother's wife and mine.

For years I thought it was only for Beth's sake that Russ would always somehow put aside his anger and become around my father more cordial, more attentive, warmer, than he usually was. In May, though, on my previous trip to Houston, I learned it was, if not his only, then his most reliable strategy for living in a white world.

After weeks of searing headaches and erratic behavior (the former her doctors diagnosed as sinus problems, the latter as depression), Beth went into a catatonic state. A cat scan showed us what we all suspected: that the breast cancer had now metastasized to her brain. With steroids, she regained consciousness only to be told that she had months, at best, to live. The day I arrived, we had our meeting with the neurosurgeon to discuss the feasibility of surgery, given the location of the tumor and my sister's history. Russ and I were sitting on one side of the bed, the doctor was standing on the other. The doctor talked for a while about the probable complications surgery would entail, and that anyway, even if it went without a hitch, the operation would give her only a few more months of life, and in what condition he couldn't say. What he could say with certainty was that the tumor couldn't be removed without damaging her brain. The Beth who went into surgery would not be the Beth who came out of it, no matter how well the operation went. I asked for more details about which mental faculties would be destroyed or compromised, and he answered courteously and at length. Then Russ asked how the cancer would progress if we did nothing, no surgery, no radiation. Instead of answering, the doctor asked, "And who are you, again?" My sister quickly interjected, "He's my husband." The doctor must have assumed that I was Beth's husband and that Russ was a family friend. An understandable mistake given that Beth and I have the same last name. Yet even after knowing who Russ was, the doctor refused to acknowledge him, the whole time looking either at me or my sister. Russ continued to participate in the discussion, his voice never once betraying any annoyance whatsoever. Throughout the conversation, he remained implacably calm and measured—determined, it seemed, in his dignified and intelligent demeanor to contradict all the assumptions that the doctor made about him. Later, I told Russ how appalled I was. In a voice I'd never heard so full of weariness, he said, "Dumb nigger till proven otherwise. That's how it always is."

For the first time, I could sense the bitterness behind the dignified façade, the rage behind the even temper. How hard Russ had to work to eat his anger and humiliation, to convert his indignation over every racial slight and innuendo into workable cordiality. And if it exhausted him to deal with clerks, doctors, mechanics, people he didn't know and whose prejudice was therefore more impersonal, easier maybe to dismiss, how much more painful and exhausting it must have been to have to overlook, put aside, ignore, and continually forgive the prejudice, the history of prejudice, within his very family. And how much more exhausting at a time like this, now that his wife was dying, and he no longer had the reserves of energy required to forbear, if not forgive. And the more we—my parents, my brother and I— grew closer as a family and closed ranks around my sister's bed, the easier, I think, it must have been for Russ to think he wasn't wanted there, or needed.

One afternoon after he visited with Beth (we usually cleared the room when he arrived so he and Beth could be alone together), Russ told me he felt trapped in a nightmare whenever he came to the hospice, a nightmare I can only understand in terms of racial anger, childhood trauma, grief, and terror over what his wife was going through, over how difficult his life would be without her. In the first ten days or so when Beth was still entirely lucid and felt wounded by his absence, I resented Russ for withdrawing from my sister at the very time that she needed him the most. By the last days, though, I felt mostly sorry for him, because it seemed to me he'd lost or given up the privilege of caring for his dying wife. At the same time, I felt ashamed too for anything we did or didn't do that might have made it easier for him to lose that privilege.

That privilege notwithstanding, by that last day we ourselves were tired of the vigil, tired for Beth, of course, but tired for ourselves as well. It had been two days since Beth had spoken. She lay in a coma, her open eyes flitting from side to side, her body at once bloated from steroids and emaciated from lack of nourishment, her swollen cheeks as hard as muscle, her shoulders, her arms, her wrists, her finger bones, especially, now nothing but twig-like points and angles. We were tired of seeing her languish, tired of the degradation we were helpless to do anything about. We were tired of our helplessness, and guilty for being tired. That we were all impatient to go home was our unspoken wish, our dirty secret.

But I had another wish as well, another dirty secret. However much I wanted to be with my sister when she died so I could comfort her as best I could, lessen what I imagined would be a terrifying loneliness, once death was imminent I also wanted, partly for selfish reasons, to see her die. Even as I feared and mourned it, I looked forward to the moment of her dying with an almost prurient curiosity. How would she look then? Where would she go? All of our notions of an afterlife seem just as implausible to me as the idea that my sister, with her unique vitality, her rich and complex and never-to-be-repeated history, would simply vanish into nothing. Wouldn't the principle of the conservation of energy contradict the fact of death as pure extinction? Wouldn't her existence have to continue in some way, if only as a fading but never completely faded energy impression on the universe? Some primitive part of me believed that if I were with her when she died, if I were vigilant enough, I'd get to peek into the mystery as the soul passed from her body out of this world into who knows where.

In the preceding days as she slipped in and out of consciousness, her wakefulness each time a little briefer, a little fainter, I grew increasingly reluctant to leave her side. I stopped going over to her house in the mornings to help Russ get Gabbi ready for camp. I stopped returning to the house in the evening hours to relax, to have a drink with Russ, to talk about the day, how Beth was doing, how my folks were holding up. And at night, I'd drive my parents back to their hotel and, instead of sitting up with them an hour or so before returning to the hospice, I'd simply drop them off and hurry back to Beth, afraid that if I weren't there she'd die without me.

Was this fascination with her dying a way to keep from thinking of the grief I'd feel once Beth was dead, the depressing blunt truth of her absence? Or was it my own death I was really thinking of, obsessing over, grieving for, as if Beth's dying enabled me to watch, experience, and understand what it would mean for me to die? What at that point was going on inside her, what portion of self, of memory, of awareness, still remained to her? Was she ready to die? Did she even know by then that she was dying? And would my presence at the moment of death itself make any difference to her?

What was she now but a page erased and written over by what each of us—out of our own particular relationship to her—was predisposed to write? Beth and I were friends as well as siblings, the "intellectuals" in the family, who had made a life of teaching, writing, learning. We were confidants, consolers, caretakers of each other's problems. And since we talked incessantly in the last two years about her illness, what it meant to die, it was consistent with our friendship that I should wonder now about her death and want to be there with her when it happened.

I was so far inside this fascination with her dying, so curious about what dying would be like, that I wondered why my parents and my brother didn't seem to feel it too. I marveled at my mother, especially since she was more involved with Beth than anyone. I'd watch her say goodbye to Beth each evening, knowing that it was more than likely Beth would not be with us by the time the morning came. She'd cry as she kissed her, but she never lingered, didn't want to linger. Unlike me, my mother had no desire whatsoever to spend the night.

As I watched her feed Beth, help turn her body from one

side to the other to make her comfortable, anticipate her needs and meet them tactfully before Beth had to ask, or just sit there holding her hand, talking quietly as she massaged Beth's forehead sometimes for hours at a time, it seemed to me at first as if Beth's illness had returned them both to a less complicated time in their relationship, to a time before Beth's tumultuous and divisive teens and early twenties, when her political rebellion as a founding member of Students for a Democratic Society in the mid-sixties, and her sexual rebellion (her boyfriend at the time was black), had badly damaged her relations with my parents. For years, my parents would have nothing to do with her, and even after they were reconciled, their relationship was always strained, muddied with ambivalence, my parents never approving of my sister's boyfriends, who were never Jewish and seldom white, my sister never entirely forgiving them for throwing her out at such a young age, for continuing not to accept her in all her differences, for continuing to cling to their idea of who she was or should be, preferring that sanitized abstraction to the person she'd become. With Beth reduced to infantlike dependency and need, it seemed as if that painful history had vanished, dissolved along with Beth's feisty independence.

And yet the more I watched the two of them, the more I realized that this intimacy wasn't a return to some less complicated time in their relationship, but the creation of something new and different, something that never existed between them and never could have existed, given who they were and the nature of their relationship.

My mother was the product of a broken home. Her parents got divorced when she was three, in the late 1920s, when divorce was anything but common. Because her mother, a successful businesswoman, traveled frequently, my mother grew up with her grandparents, becoming in effect a younger sibling to her aunts and uncles, none of whom had much respect for her father, who, as a whole-sale meat dealer, never amounted to much in their eyes. As if it happened only yesterday, not more than sixty years ago, my mother still bitterly recalls how her aunts would tease her constantly about her father. Whenever they would quarrel, whenever my mother would upset her aunts in any way, they'd tell her she was selfish like her father, or stupid like her father, that her mother had no business marrying such a bum. Her reaction to this teasing was not only to defend her father, but to idealize him as a kind, sweet man ("He'd never hurt a fly"). In so doing, she asserted her independence from their image of him and, even more important, from what they thought of her.

In compensation for that childhood pain, my mother demanded of her husband and her children a degree of devotion that none of us could ever satisfy. It almost seemed that by insisting we conform to her impossible ideal of how a family ought to be, she ensured that we would disappoint her, as if the sense of grievance that she carried into her relationship with us was so extreme she felt compelled to manufacture situations that would justify it.

As the eldest child and only daughter, Beth became the target of our mother's highest hopes and bitterest disappointments. In her stubbornness and independence, Beth, in fact, was too much like her mother to submit to her. The more Ma demanded of her, the more she either bristled or withdrew. My mother tells a story about Beth as a nine-year-old that I think captures the misunderstandings and contentions of their relationship. Beth was at summer camp. It was the first time she'd ever been away from home for any length of time. Halfway through the summer, on visiting day, my parents arrived. The way my mother tells the story, she and Dad are standing with several other parents; they're looking for Beth. My mother can't wait to see her. Everywhere children are running excitedly into their parents' arms, but Beth is nowhere in sight. At last they find her, among some other kids, and when my mother calls her name, Beth says "Oh, hi," and walks off with another girl. Usually in response to something Beth did as an adult that either hurt or disappointed her, my mother would use this story to illustrate how little family feeling Beth possessed, even as a child; how she always cared more for her friends than for her parents. Beth and I never discussed this story (I doubt that she remembered the incident, or even knew Ma told it as the representative anecdote about her daughter). Who knows what Beth was feeling when she heard Ma call her name? Maybe she was distracted, or unwell, or maybe, since the other girl's parents hadn't yet arrived, Beth didn't want to hurt her feelings by leaving her for Ma and Dad. Whatever the reason, I know that Ma was probably unable to disguise how hurt she felt, and that in response to the disappointment Ma was unable not to show, Beth probably grew more detached and incommunicable, her coldness now the only way she could protect her own identity against Ma's overwhelming need for her to be the perfect daughter.

And yet if Beth was like her mother in her stubbornness and independence, by the time she reached her late teens and early twenties she was also like her mother in having been abandoned by her parents. And that similar history predisposed them both, I think, to put the worst construction on each other's actions.

That sad and complicated history came to an end, it seemed, when Beth got sick. Ironically, her cancer enabled them to get beyond the contest for autonomy and self-definition that the two of them had been compelled to wage, as daughters, as mothers, as wives, and more generally as women independent of these familial roles. It was as if her illness permitted them both to be more generous, more imaginative than they had ever been before. Because my mother knew Beth had no choice but to accept the care she had to give, she gave it tactfully, respectfully, so that it came as much as possible without the stigma of submission. And Beth, in turn, accepted gratefully everything Ma tried to do, because she knew how painful it would be if it were Gabbi dying, and she caring for her daughter the way her mother now cared for her. What seemed most remarkable was the mutual forbearance, restraint, and profound courtesy in their attentions to each other. My mother could have overwhelmed my sister with maternal care; Beth's abject neediness would have justified it. My sister could have accepted grudgingly or bitterly the care she couldn't do without, compensating for the humiliation of her helplessness with understandable impatience, irritability, anger. Neither of them did.

The unique maturity of their relationship was nowhere more apparent than in the last few days when Beth, still conscious, stopped asking for food or liquid, and my mother stopped offering, even though she knew not getting her to eat or drink would hasten her death. That she could let go of her daughter and, once Beth lost consciousness, tell her it was all right to die, to take God's hand, was the ultimate expression of the intimacy the two of them had finally achieved. That they had achieved it is why, I think, my mother had no desire to be there with her daughter when she died. The very way she'd been with Beth throughout each day of those last four weeks was how she'd said goodbye, and having said it she'd done everything that it was possible for her to do.

I was thinking about all of this that last day as I lay on the floor beside my sister's bed. I was thinking about Russ and Beth, Beth and my mother, Beth and me, always Beth in relation to one of us. It had been two days now since she had spoken, only a faint wheeze or whimper coming from her chest. In the days before she slipped into the coma, every now and then I'd ask her how she was feeling, what she was thinking of. "Nothing," she'd murmur, "absolutely nothing." The massive amounts of morphine needed to eat up the pain had left her either deeply asleep or drifting in a sort of waking dream. Yet on the morning of the last day she had spoken, she woke and told my mother, "I think I'm getting better." An hour later, the doctor asked her if she was okay, and she said, "I think I'm okay somewhere inside." And when the nurse arrived to change her urine bag, Beth answered her cheery "Hi Beth!" with "I want to get out of here."

The nurse thought "here" meant the hospice, that Beth was asking to go home. But I was certain that it meant the body that betrayed her, that she felt better, "okay somewhere inside," because she knew that death was near and she was ready for it. Those were the last words she had spoken. And two days later she was still alive. The whimpering in her chest had persisted for twelve hours now. All through the night and morning, it was horrible to listen to because I couldn't tell, and the nurses couldn't tell me, if it was just some physiological event, the onset of the death rattle, or if it meant that Beth was trying unsuccessfully to tell us something, to communicate one last time. I was thinking as I lay there, before the vision came, of how completely inaccessible my sister was to all of us as the life within her petered out. The nurses told us that the hearing is the last to go, that we should still be careful of what we said around her. But did she hear us? And though unable to communicate, did she still feel in our presence some remnant of who she'd been for each of us? And was there, then, some pressure to continue being, conforming to, the person we each of us unconsciously still needed her to be? And was that whimper then some feeble protest that she was tired of us all, that she wanted to be left alone? Or did it simply mean that her life had thoroughly dissolved past her identity into the mere machinery of slowing heart and lung?

Flat on my back, my feet up on a chair, my eyes closed, suddenly I saw my sister. She was lying on a made bed, the covers under her. She looked like her old self, only thinner than she'd ever been, sleeker, and she was dressed like a dancer, a Rockette, in black tights, black shirt, and vest, the costume all awash in sequins, her top hat tilted stylishly down to just above her eyes. She was smiling not at me but in my direction, as if I'd only accidentally crossed the path of her attention—like someone you think is greeting you and whom you've therefore waved and smiled at, and then discover as she nears that she has all along been looking past you, at someone else, she doesn't know that you exist. The smile widened. It went on widening into a grotesque Cheshire cat smile, and suddenly I realized that what I thought had been a smile was only flesh disintegrating, disappearing like an ebbing tide beyond her lips and cheeks, up over the forehead, down her neck, into the collar of her black shirt, till just the skull lay on the pillow, the top hat now slumped forward over the eye sockets, the tight-fitting clothes now loose and billowy as they settled to the bones that could have been anybody's.

"Aw shit," the black taxi driver at Hobby Airport said when I told him I was going to St. Luke's Hospital. "A piss-ass fare ain't worth the time I waited."

"Gee, I'm sorry," I said as I got into the taxi. Then to prove I had a legitimate reason for going to St. Luke's instead of to some more lucrative destination I added, "My sister's sick. She's dying."

"Ain't your fault, man. Don't worry about it."

It took a moment before I realized he was referring to the money he wouldn't make, not to my sister.

I felt ashamed for mentioning Beth, for using her illness to appease the anger of a disgruntled cabbie, just so I wouldn't have to feel uncomfortable about the measly fare. Yet this was just an especially pure expression of what I feel whenever I get into a taxi, which is why I don't like taking them. Out of some misplaced egalitarian anxiety, I find myself compelled to apologize in some way to those whom I pay to serve me. I usually do this with small talk and charm. By entertaining the driver, by demonstrating interest in his life, I sugarcoat—to myself if not to him—the inequality of our positions. This is the flip side of the anxiety I felt when I was hacking some twenty-five years ago. In those days, I made a point of entertaining every fare. Through wit and intelligence I tried to show that I was more than just a cabbie, that, my menial position notwithstanding, I was just as interesting and complex a human being as those who hired me. The more engaged they were by what I'd tell them, the more level seemed the playing field between us.

So from either side of the bullet-proof Plexiglas partition, I felt, still feel, the nervous and exhausting need to prove myself, alleviate an insecurity of one kind or another. Even on this day, even now, going to see my dying sister.

The night before when Russ called to say I ought to come as quickly as possible, that Beth was in terrible shape, that he was sure the cancer had spread again, he told me, in tears, that he didn't think I'd recognize her, even though I'd been there only six weeks earlier. He said that she was now completely bald from the radiation and the radio surgery, and that her body, her face especially, was warped and bloated from the steroids. He also told me that she was mostly out of it, with all the morphine she was taking. Two weeks before when my mother had gone out to visit, she too had said that Beth looked awful—her face so swollen that her nose was hardly visible, no larger than a dot. When I mentioned my mother's comment to Russ, he said as bad as Beth looked fourteen days ago, she looks a thousand times worse now.

I was terrified that she would die before I got there. And just as terrified that she would still be living. So added to my usual taxi-induced anxiety over class and status was my terror over what I'd find when I reached my sister's room, a terror that made me even more nervous and talkative than usual.

I'd noticed the GO ROCKETS sticker on the cab's rear bumper, so once we pulled out into traffic I asked him if he was a Rockets fan and had he watched the finals. He was a fan, he said, but he was too busy bustin' his ass to make a living to catch any of the games.

"Well," I replied, ignoring the aggrieved tone, "I guess

everybody got caught up in the excitement. My sister's only lived here five years and she's become a big fan of the Rockets."

"That so."

"How long have you been living here in Houston?"

"About twenty years."

"Where you from originally?"

"Lansing, Michigan."

"No kidding." I said, leaning forward. "That's where my sister moved here from. She went to MSU."

"So did I. Played safety on the football team."

"What year did you graduate?"

"'65."

"So you were on the national championship team?"

"Damn right."

"I can't believe it. My sister knew a lot of the players— Bubba Smith, Mike Webster, Gene Washington. She even got me an autographed football. Everyone signed it, I bet your name's on it too. Maybe you know Beth, Beth Shapiro?"

"Didn't start," he said by way of answer. "Only the starters got to sign those balls."

I told him that my sister had settled in Lansing after college, that she worked in the library, and over the years did a lot of work for the Athletic Department. She had even tutored Magic Johnson during his sophomore year, the year the Spartans won the NCAA tournament. She and the coach, Judd Heathcote, were friends, I told him, Judd was one of the first people to call her, back in May, when word got out that she was terminally ill.

He didn't so much as nod at or acknowledge this. When the silence got too awkward for me, I asked him what it was that made him move from Lansing. Did he have family here in Houston?

Then he began to talk. He said it was family trouble that

made him leave home in the early seventies. He said his sister had worked at the Lansing Oldsmobile plant and had gotten him a job there when he left school. A few years later, she was killed one afternoon at work when a forklift operator had accidentally run her over. He wanted the family to sue the pants off Oldsmobile, since the guy who killed his sister had a history of drinking on the job, and he was drunk that afternoon, but his parents just wanted to put the whole sorry mess behind them. They accepted the few diddly-squat thousand dollars that the company offered. He was so mad at everyone, at Oldsmobile, at his parents, at the forklift operator who, aside from being fired, never really paid for what he'd done, that he decided he couldn't live in Lansing any longer and moved down here where, he was told, the cost of living was cheap, the weather warm, and there were good jobs to be had in the oil industry. When I asked him if Houston turned out to be all that he expected, he just said, "The weather's hot as shit."

"What a sad story," I offered lamely, and he replied, "You got that right." I didn't know what else to say. This story was a little too personal for the ersatz intimacy I tried to cultivate, and the sadness of it, too, was too close to my own, too close to what I wanted for the moment not to think about. Maybe that's why he told it—to equalize our situations so I couldn't think that I was any more deserving of his sympathy than he was of mine. Maybe, tired of my pretense of respect and curiosity, he knew the story would shut me up.

I sat back and watched the Astrodome come into view, and then the first tall buildings of the Texas Medical Center, somewhere in the middle of which my sister lay. I imagined myself entering her room, and telling her about the remarkable coincidence of being driven from the airport by an ex-Spartan, someone she maybe knew. I imagined that we'd reminisce about the '64 championship team, and the infamous showdown with Notre Dame when Ara Parsegian settled for the tie, deciding to kick the extra point instead of going for two after the Irish scored a touchdown in the closing seconds. I tried to think through in detail what we would say to one another, what she would look like, how I'd react. I tried to picture everything, worry every possibility into vivid focus, so I could think that I was ready for whatever was about to meet me, though the more elaborately I imagined what I'd say, scripting in advance my stories, witticisms, questions about how or what Beth felt, the less prepared and more afraid I felt.

We pulled up before the main entrance of the hospital. The fare was twenty-four dollars. As I pulled out my wallet, the driver asked, "So what do you think of the trial?"

"Sorry?"

"The trial, man," he repeated. "You know, O. J., Nicole, Mark Fuhrman."

Assuming he believed O. J. was innocent and framed by a racist cop, and not wanting to confirm what I assumed he assumed I thought, I said my sister's married to a black man. And from what I've seen of their life, especially here in Houston, I had no trouble believing the police would want to frame him. Anyway, it seemed unlikely that he could have killed Nicole and Ron Goldman and still gotten back to his house and cleaned himself up in time to meet the limo.

"Takes no time to cut somebody," he said. He turned around to face me. "Say you don't know I'm here. And I come up behind you. How long you think I need to slit your throat?"

I gave him thirty dollars. I said keep the change. "No problem," he replied, as if I'd asked him for a favor.

"Hey," he called out as I hurried from the cab. "Been where you are, man. Take care."

*   *   *   *

*H*owever much I tried envisioning Beth as Russ described her, I still saw Beth when I pictured her. I saw the sister whom I had always known. And when I imagined entering her room, I saw her seeing me, smiling as she always did when I'd arrive, ready and eager to be entertained—even under the most trying circumstances. But the woman sitting on the edge of her bed, facing the door as I came in, was no one I'd ever seen before. It wasn't the sparse hairs growing like a baby's on her otherwise bald head, or even the horrid distension of her body, the face not only swollen but pulled this way and that, as if reflected in a fun-house mirror. What frightened me most of all was the combination of recognition in her eyes and utter lack of affect as she looked up when the young woman standing next to her said, "Oh, look, Beth, you have a visitor." "I want to lie down," was all she moaned in answer. Beth was winded, and in terrible pain. Unable to hold herself erect, she leaned against the woman, grimacing as the woman slowly eased her back into the bed.

In a voice of professional good cheer, the woman told me she was the physical therapist assigned to Beth. They'd just finished a "terrific" session which consisted of Beth walking with the aid of a walker from her bed to the door of her room and back, a distance of maybe ten feet in all. With the affectionate condescension of a teacher talking to a parent in the presence of the child she's praising, the therapist said Beth did a wonderful job, and that tomorrow they'd try going even farther.

Beth looked as if she'd run the marathon. She was breathing heavily, groaning in pain whenever she moved an arm or leg. Given how miserable she was, and how much pain it caused her to exert herself in any way, I wondered whether physical therapy would do more harm than good. The therapist must have seen the skepticism on my face, for she immediately explained that getting up and about would cut down on the chance of bedsores, and that the stimulation would be just the thing for her depression. No, I said, a cure for cancer would be just the thing for that. She picked up her clipboard. "I'll be back tomorrow, Beth," she smiled. Then saying to me, "Enjoy your visit," she left the room.

Barely a moment later, the male nurse arrived to give Beth a shot of morphine. "Okay, sweetheart," he said, "this ought to make you comfortable." She groaned as he turned her over on her side, administered the shot to her left buttock. Then he rolled her back. "That ought to do it, sweetheart. Sweet dreams." He was in his late twenties. A big well-built man with a pencil-thin mustache, slicked-back hair. Vegas lounge singer as nurse. The kind of man my sister would have detested. She'd have hated the of-course-I'm-irresistible condescension in the cutesy tone, the endearments a little too well-oiled, the competence too brusque. But as he pulled the covers back up over her and, winking, said, "Catch ya later, honey," she smiled at him, much to my surprise, and thanked him. I was going to make some snide remark about the Wayne Newton look-alike, but Beth was sleeping already by the time he left.

As of last night, Russ still didn't know why Beth was in such terrible shape. The oncologist had done a spinal tap earlier in the week. Now it was Friday and he still hadn't returned any of Russ's calls. Since the MRI indicated that the tumor hadn't spread, that it was one-third the size it was back in May before the radio surgery, it was still a mystery to her doctors why her headaches had returned, why her back ached, why she couldn't stand without dizziness. Looking at her, I didn't need a test to tell me what was wrong. Beth was really dying now; she seemed already dead in large part, her body taken from her, replaced with this freakish stranger, her spirit reduced to creaturely distress so pure and unremitting that it made her cry out even as she slept. I knew I ought to take her hand, massage her neck and forehead, touch her in some soothing way, but I couldn't move.

It shames me to say this now, but I couldn't touch her. I was afraid to. Beth and I were close friends, as well as siblings. Our intimacy, though, was based in language, wit, freewheeling conversation, not physical contact. There was never much of that between any of us in the family. As I stood there, I realized how much our intimacy relied on words, on measured speech. Even at times of crisis, we always kept up the appearance of control over ourselves and of our circumstances. We seldom broke down in each other's company. And on the rare occasions when we did, we were always quick to joke about it afterward, or if not joke about it, then talk through the trouble and, by talking, show that we understood what we were going through and therefore were superior to even the most difficult emotions, never entirely possessed by them. Our way of nurturing one another was to give advice, suggestions, sympathy. To touch her now, I felt, would be to touch the brute, unvarnished fact of her dying; it would be to face her, as she was now, without a busy gloss of words between us. Talking was for us a kind of doing, and where there was nothing left to do, talk gave us the illusion of doing, the illusion of solving, of working through, of planning or puzzling. Just to be with her now in silence, to take her hand, to touch her and not say anything, was to be intolerably present to her intolerable pain.

Weakly, I asked, What's wrong, Beth? Is there anything I can do? Over and over I asked her this, could not stop asking this, even though I knew there was nothing to do, nothing to say, that Beth was so far gone in her own suffering she probably didn't even know that I was there. Or if she did know, she was nonetheless beyond the reach of anything I could give her.

I sat down in the recliner next to her bed. The TV's remote control dangled from the guardrail. I picked it up, turned on the TV, surfed through all the channels, then turned it off again. The clock on the wall read 2:30. Russ was to pick me up before the main entrance at five. Two and a half hours to go. I switched off the overhead light. I lay back, my hand clutching the guardrail, as if to brace myself against expected turbulence. Wanting to sleep too much to think I would, I closed my eyes. With a start I woke two hours later and discovered that while I was sleeping Beth had taken up my hand in hers. Wide awake, I sat there in the dark room for a little while longer, Beth now sleeping peacefully beside me, my hand in hers, till it was time for me to go.

* * * *

Beth, Russ, and Gabbi were supposed to fly to Michigan next Wednesday, so that Beth could say goodbye to all her many friends there. The trip would coincide with her birthday on the 18th of July, and Russ had planned a huge bash. I was going to meet them there over the weekend, and then bring Beth and Gabbi back to Chapel Hill for a visit with my family. And then in August, Della, I, and the kids planned to come to Houston for a week. That was how Beth wanted to spend her last summer in the world.

Almost as soon as I got into Russ's car, I told him I didn't see how Beth was going to go to Michigan. "She's more resilient than she looks," he said. She'd better be, I thought, because if she weren't she'd be lucky to live out the week. Russ had arranged for Gabbi to spend the night at a friend's house. He wanted to see his friend Bill Redwine. A cardiologist, Bill would get through to Beth's oncologist, if anybody could. Russ had been calling the oncologist all week to find out what, if anything, the spinal tap had revealed. But the doctor hadn't called him back. He was tired of waiting, tired of being put on hold, tired of not knowing.

Russ knew Bill through his wife, Shirley, Rice University's legal counselor. Russ, an administrator in the university's human resource office, had worked with Shirley on a number of projects, and they'd become good friends. Bill hadn't gotten home yet, but Shirley told us to make ourselves comfortable. She got us drinks, and we sat and chatted awkwardly for I don't know how long. I'd been to their house the summer before when I came to town to help Russ with Gabbi while Beth recovered from her stem cell transplant. That procedure culminated six harrowing months of treatment that included a mastectomy, chemotherapy, and radiation. The stem cell transplant, her oncologist said, was an insurance policy against recurrence. If successful, Beth would have a better than 50 percent chance of living for another five years.

The Redwines live almost directly across the street from the football stadium. Over the July Fourth weekend, toward the end of Beth's isolation, the Eagles held a concert in the stadium, and the Redwines invited a bunch of friends to their house to hear the music from their backyard. It was a lovely party. The pleasure of it was intensified for me and Russ by the apparent success of Beth's procedure. She'd survived the transplant. The latest bone scan showed her body clean of cancer, and she would soon be coming home.

As we waited for Bill, we talked about that party as if it were ancient history. We talked about my children, about the weather and how dreadful it had been, we talked about the Rockets. Soon we ran out of things to talk about, Shirley excused herself, and Russ and I sat in silence until Bill came home.

We described Beth's symptoms to him. It was clear, he told us, that the cancer had spread to her meninges, that's the only explanation for all her recent suffering. What does that mean? Russ asked. And Bill said, if he was right, then we should get Beth discharged from the hospital and into hospice care as soon as possible. Medically, there was nothing else to be done for her except to make her comfortable. He said he'd call the oncologist and see what he could find out. He went into the kitchen. From the living room where we were sitting, we could hear Bill leave a message on the doctor's pager. No sooner had he hung up than the phone rang. It had taken him, a fellow doctor, all of thirty seconds to get hold of the oncologist. We could hear him say that he was calling about Beth Shapiro, then he was quiet for a few seconds, and when he said, Yes, that's just what I suspected, Russ and I began to cry. Shirley had returned with a box of tissues. Bill told us when he got off the phone that the tests had confirmed that the cancer had spread up through the spinal column, that Beth had carcinomic meningitis, tumors on the lining of her brain. The oncologist had already been to see Beth, and had told her the news. He'd presented her with a choice of either doing nothing or taking orally one last form of treatment, a pill of some kind that would sicken but not kill the new tumors. Beth had opted for the treatment, Bill informed us, and the doctor had already given it to her.

I was furious. The doctor must have come just after I had left. That he would break the news to Beth while she was by herself without her family there to comfort her was bad enough; but to present her with a choice of treatments when she was barely lucid was outrageous. Son of a bitch, I said. Bill, not wanting, I guess, to speak ill of a fellow doctor, didn't respond except to say, again, that we should think about hospice care. Beth would have days, possibly weeks, but not months to live. And all we could do for her now was try to make her comfortable. The hospice at the Texas Medical Center was excellent at what he called pain management, much better than the hospital. He said he was sorry.

We rushed back to St. Luke's to see how Beth was doing.

She was asleep by the time we got there. Russ said that for the last few days she'd been either delirious with pain, or zonked out on morphine. Between those two states there was usually a short but unpredictable period just after the morphine had taken effect, yet before it knocked her out, when she was lucid enough to have a conversation. She was out cold now, and anyway visiting hours were almost over, so we went home.

Back at the house, I phoned my parents. My mother responded to the news as if she'd been expecting it. Her readiness was like a soldier's on the verge of battle, fearful but too well trained to show it. She didn't cry or curse but simply said that she and Dad would fly out as soon as possible, and that I ought to find them a hotel near the hospice.

*　　*　　*　　*

Beth was awake when I arrived at her room the next morning.

"Ma and Dad are coming, Beth. They'll be here on Tuesday."

"Why?" she said. "Ma was just here a couple of weeks ago."

"You know, they want to see you."

"Where are they going to stay?"

"I got them a room at the Holiday Inn."

"Oh God," she laughed, "Ma's gonna complain like she did in May. Not enough closet space."

"I don't think so, Beth. Not this time."

"And why should this time be any different?"

I didn't know what to answer. Either Beth was taking the bad news remarkably well or she'd forgotten it.

"Besides," she continued, "I'm supposed to leave for Michigan on Wednesday."

"Beth," I said sadly, "you're in no condition to travel. You can hardly stand up."

"Well, I don't know. Maybe I'll feel better in a day or two. Anyway, even if I don't, Russ and Gabbi should still go. Russ really needs to get away."

"I don't think he'll want to go without you, not at a time like this."

"Why? What's gonna happen to me in here? And if I'm well enough to go home, even if I can't travel, I could use the time alone, to clean up a little, pay bills, straighten out the accounts, they're such a mess."

"Beth, did Dr. P. come see you yesterday?"

"I don't know if it was yesterday or this morning. I've completely lost track of time."

"What did he tell you?"

"Not much," she lamented. "He doesn't like seeing me anymore."

"What do you mean?"

"Oh, you know, after the stem cell transplant, when I was doing well, he was all smiles. He used to say he was so proud of me, I was his best patient. It depresses him to see me now, I think. He's always so glum."

"So did he tell you anything?"

"No," she said, "what's he going to tell me?"

"Nothing, I guess. I was just thinking if he'd gotten back the test results, we'd have a better sense of what you can and can't do."

Her head began to hurt. The pain came on suddenly and ferociously. I got the nurse, and he gave her a shot of morphine. While it took effect, she asked me to massage her forehead. And as I massaged her, she said dreamily, until she slipped into unconsciousness, that just this morning she had made an appointment for Gabbi to get a haircut in ten days when they got back from Michigan and Chapel Hill, and that she was dead set on taking her herself because she didn't think Gabbi would go with Russ and anyway Russ probably didn't know where the hair salon was located, and she had all the bills to do, they really needed an accountant, she was so tired of doing everything herself.

*　　*　　*　　*

Beth had completely forgotten what Doctor P. had told her. Was it the morphine or the tumor or some combination of the two that made her forget? Would her memory worsen as the days passed, so that even if we told her again that she was dying, she'd forget again, and again have to be told? Or should we not tell her at all, and let her spend what time she had left thinking God knows what about her situation? Russ said we had to tell her, this time at least, and from then on we'd just take our cues from her, and treat whatever reality she inhabited as the only one.

We had a one o'clock appointment at the hospice, and a three o'clock appointment at the funeral home to pick out Beth's urn, and start the paperwork going for the death certificates, copies of which I'd need in order to cancel without penalty the various airline tickets we had purchased for the trips we'd planned to Michigan and Houston, and so I myself could get the bereavement rate on my flight here. It was an odd blessing to have so many petty affairs to tend to in the middle of this unbearable sorrow. This day, in fact, would be the beginning of interminable hours of paperwork, hours on the phone, hours of waiting in offices of one kind or another, dealing with ticket agents, insurance companies, government bureaucrats; the beginning of my education in both the sacred and profane dimensions of what it means for a middle-class American to die. Eventually, I'd find the business side of dying exhaustingly tedious. But today I happily sought refuge in it, especially since I knew that when we'd gotten these appointments out of the way we'd have to face my sister with the terrible news.

*　　*　　*　　*

The hospice director, a woman whose name I've forgotten, met us at the front door and took us on a tour of the facility. An old Tudor-style mansion, the hospice consisted of two floors of rooms, and a third floor under construction. There was a large garden in the back, with paths winding among flowerbeds and small pools, at one end a quaint gazebo, at the other a small playground for children. The rooms too were very large, and each had a couch in it that opened into a double bed, in case any family members wanted to spend the night. The rooms, the director informed us, could accommodate almost anything from home that the patient wanted or the family needed, including pets. Russ's first comment as we walked through the garden was that Gabbi would be comfortable spending time here, she could bring her friends, or her dog, Magic, and probably wouldn't get as antsy as she did in the hospital.

We reentered the building through a far door on the other side of the garden, and there in the foyer, sitting on a bench, was a young woman in a radiant white wedding dress replete with an elaborate train. Beside her sat the groom in a tuxedo. For a moment I thought I'd stumbled into a Fellini film. The hospice director explained that the bride was the granddaughter of one of the patients here, that the actual wedding was being held in August, but that the grandmother wasn't going to make it, that she had only days at best to live, so the family arranged a mock wedding to take place in the woman's room that afternoon. The woman, though, had gotten terribly sick as the ceremony began, and the nurses were tending to her.

The bride and groom sat side by side. Not even glancing at us as we passed, they stared straight ahead at nothing, looking bored, impatient, put out. Clearly the mock ceremony wasn't their idea. Nevertheless, the image of them followed me into the brightly lit hallway busy with nurses going in and out of rooms, with families in different stages of their own grieving, with the dying I glimpsed as this or that door opened or closed, and the image, juxtaposed with what I now saw around me, had the disorienting force of revelation.

Life is pitiless in its profound complexity, its indifferent richness. Because my sister was dying, I wanted everyone to grieve. I wanted life to stand still and acknowledge sorrowfully the loss of my sister, someone without whom my own life was unthinkable. But from moment to moment, even I wasn't merely grieving. Or the grief itself wasn't monolithic; it didn't exclude other emotions or perceptions. The image of the bride and groom at the threshold of the hospice made me remember what had happened the night before when I'd just learned from Bill Redwine the truth of Beth's condition. After we left Bill's house and headed over to the hospital, by habit Russ turned on the radio, which happened to be set to Gabbi's favorite country and western station. We heard Hank Williams singing in a mournful, woozy twang, "And I'm so lonesome I could die." Russ and I looked at each other, tears streaming down our faces. "How about a station that plays show tunes," I offered, and we laughed the whole way to the hospital.

We finished our business at the hospice, we inspected the room that Beth would have, we filled out the appropriate forms and arranged for Beth to be moved on Tuesday. Then we drove across town to the funeral home, where we filled out more forms to arrange for the cremation and the death certificate. Then we picked out Beth's urn, a moderately priced bronze vessel that resembled an ancient Greek amphora. We did all this matter-of-factly, numbly, never actually connecting the urn we held or the forms we signed to the incineration of my sister's body and the ashes that would fill the cool urn in our hands in just a matter of days.

*   *   *   *

*B*eth was awake and lucid when we arrived at her room. Russ sat in the chair next to her bed, I stood on the other side. He asked her the question I had asked the night before, if she remembered Dr. P.'s visit. And Beth told him what she had told me, that she couldn't remember when it was he visited, and that he told her nothing.

"Beth," he said, taking her hand, "the cancer has spread."

"What do you mean?" she asked.

"You have tumors on the lining of your brain. There's cancer in your spinal column. There's nothing we can do now."

"How much time do I have?"

"Days, maybe weeks, that's all."

"Oh," Beth moaned, "that's terrible. Does Gabbi know?"

"I haven't told her yet," Russ said, barely above a whisper.

"Have you told Ma and Dad?" she asked me.

"Yes, of course, they'll be here Tuesday."

"But I haven't gotten anything done." Beth wailed, like a child whose parents won't let her have her way. "I haven't written my obituary, or straightened out the insurance, or planned the memorial service."

"We'll take care of all that, Beth," I said. "You don't need to worry about those things."

"We're going to move you to the hospice," Russ added. "It's just lovely there, the rooms are spacious, Gabbi'll be able to visit anytime she wants, and there's plenty for her to do. We can even bring Magic. And they'll keep you comfortable. That's what they're good at."

Still holding Russ's hand, she reached up for mine. We stayed like that for a minute or two in silence.

"Do you want me to bring your Bible?" Russ asked.

"No," Beth said now somewhat dreamily. "I'm too skeptical for that."

"What can I do for you?" I asked. "Do you want anything?"

"I want to see my daughter graduate from high school," she said. "But that's not going to happen, is it?"

I felt accused by the comment, accused and stupid because I also knew that there was nothing I or anyone could say in answer to the unredeemable anguish in her voice. Yet I had to break the silence. I had to ripple the surface of the moment that showed too clearly the darkness of its own depths.

"Hey Beth," I said, too cheerfully, "you know the cabbie who drove me in from the airport yesterday actually moved here from Lansing twenty years ago. What a coincidence, huh? He even claimed he'd been a defensive back on the MSU national championship team!"

"Really?" Beth answered, genuinely interested, which shouldn't have surprised me, given her passion for sports. She even did her doctoral work at MSU on the sociology of collegiate athletics.

"Yeah, but I don't know if he was telling the truth. When I asked him if he'd signed those footballs, you know, like the one you got me, he said he never saw much action, and that only the starters got to sign them."

"That's true," she said, sleepily, her eyes now closed. "Only the starters signed those balls."

"Well, maybe he was telling the truth. I thought he was just trying to get a bigger tip."

"Could've been both," Beth murmured. "Anyway, what was his name? Maybe I knew him."

Beth drifted off to sleep before I had a chance to answer, which was just as well, since I realized only then that I never actually learned the driver's name. I never thought to ask him who he was.

*I*t didn't surprise me when Beth said she was too skeptical to read the Bible. As a child she'd been more religious, or more dutiful about religion, than anyone else in the family, but from her twenties on, she'd been a fire-breathing radical, one of the founding members of SDS on the Michigan State University campus in the mid-sixties, and even after her radicalism cooled, and she became associate director of the MSU library, running (so she liked to joked) the very institution she once at an SDS meeting considered burning down, she never lost her zeal for politics. Whenever I'd visit, she was constantly introducing me to community organizers, social workers, civil rights activists with whom she'd worked on this or that campaign. No matter how long it had been since she had seen me, or how briefly I was staying, I'd spend most of the visit waiting for her as she ran from one grassroots organization meeting to another. The only times, it seemed, that I would warrant her complete attention were times of personal trouble: when my first wife and I broke up, for instance, or when I fell ill with Graves disease. In the early seventies especially, I used to tease her that she cared about me only when I was depressed or beaten down enough to distract her from the victims of American capitalism.

Only after Gabbi was born did she renew her interest in

Judaism, but even then it was Judaism's social and cultural dimensions that drew her, not any appetite for some transcendent truth. She turned back to the Jewish tradition not in order to glorify the creator but to provide her daughter with a cultural identity alternative to those offered by the mass media. The spirit world for Beth was first and foremost a communal world, which explains not only her appetite for politics, and her remarkably extended web of friendships and affiliations, but also her mania for basketball and football. For it was less the game itself she loved than the social experience of watching it with others, the more the better. She used to say that her happiest childhood memories were of getting into our parents' bed on Sunday afternoons and watching football with David, me, and Dad. I think in her mind sports became synonymous with family intimacy, an intimacy that sadly grew less frequent as she grew older. For Beth, the stadium or arena was like a temple, a sacred space in which everyone, at least for the duration of the game, can slip free of the profane worries and concerns of everyday existence and merge with strangers into a communal mind that's moved by a single passion. A kind of family bed writ large. The transcendence she believed in, in other words, was horizontal, not vertical.

This changed to some extent when she was told in May that she had only months to live. One of the first things we did when she was well enough to leave the hospital was visit with the rabbi of her synagogue. Ever practical, Beth wanted to set in place the arrangements for her funeral and memorial service. She wanted to make sure that Rabbi Michaels would preside over the service, and that her decision to be cremated was consistent with the practices of Reform Judaism. She also wanted to get Gabbi enrolled in Sunday school.

After we got these practicalities out of the way, the rabbi asked Beth if she was ready to die. In keeping with her Jewish heritage, she answered his question with a question of her own: "Are you?" To his credit, the rabbi, a handsome, young-looking man in his early forties, said he wasn't, no, there was too much in his life he hadn't yet accomplished. And then of course there were his children, whom he wanted to see grow up. His honesty, painful as it was for all of us to hear, was like a breath of fresh but very chilly air, stinging and enlivening all at once. It seemed to put us all at ease. Beth said that what she most regretted and most feared was her absence from her daughter's life. Yet she could face the prospect of that absence less fearfully and sorrowfully if she knew that she'd done all she could for Gabbi in what time they'd had together. She'd be more at peace if she could know that Russ and Gabbi would be all right after her death. And toward that end, she wanted to find a nanny for Gabbi, now, and to hire an accountant to help Russ with the household bills, and to get her papers in order.

"Well," the rabbi said, "if that's what will give you peace, then be sure to do it. You've already taught your daughter and everyone who knows you so much in the way you've lived. Now what you have to do is teach them how to die."

Impatiently, I listened to their conversation. Beth, I knew, needed more from the rabbi than just advice about practicalities on behalf of others. Faced with her own extinction, she had terrors, private terrors, that needed solacing. While waiting for the rabbi to finish up an earlier appointment, we had browsed through the library at the synagogue. Most of the books Beth looked at had to do with Jewish answers to the question of what happens to us after we die. Clearly she wanted to learn about the other world, what Judaism had to say about the soul after the death of the body. She seemed self-conscious, though, even embarrassed, about this curiosity. I watched her almost secretively pull down and scan through those books, and then return them to the shelf before anyone noticed. Did she feel that she didn't deserve such consolation now, that she hadn't earned it by living a religious life? Or that to seek it only now that she was dying would have contradicted who she'd always been, and how she'd lived? She'd always prided herself on her bluntness and realism and practicality, on her unflinching devotion to the truth, however bleak or grim. Maybe she felt that seeking an eleventh-hour refuge from the truth of her mortality in some consoling myth would have amounted to a betrayal of her essential self.

Or maybe this self-consciousness was yet another expression of her lifelong reluctance to act on her own behalf, to put her own needs first before the needs of others, to take something for herself. Effectual, assertive, and supremely confident in her professional life, when it came to personal matters Beth had very little confidence. She wrongly assumed that in a roomful of people she'd always be the least deserving of attention. Like the drunkard who goes from doctor to doctor until he finds one that tells him that he doesn't have a drinking problem, Beth put more stock in the opinion of those few people who didn't like her than in the many who did. She had a wonderful sense of humor, yet she was much more comfortable in the audience laughing at someone else's joke than in the spotlight telling one herself, just as in her friendships she was much more comfortable doing for others than having things done for her.

I'd never realized the full extent of this abiding insecurity until those first days after we learned that Beth had only months to live. Devastated as she was by the news, she was also exhilarated by the attention others gave her. While she was in the hospital, friends and colleagues never left her side. She received cards and letters from people all over the country. She'd even gotten a call from Judd Heathcote, the coach of the MSU basketball team. She was surprised by this attention, and sadly delighted by it, delighted to have her sense of herself, her doubts and uncertainties, so thoroughly and convincingly contradicted. Yet look at what it took to convince her that she was worthy to be loved and cared for.

And even now, it seemed to me, she couldn't bring herself to ask the rabbi for some personal reassurance, to help her with the terrifying loneliness she must have felt as she readied herself for dying. If she weren't going to ask the rabbi to help diminish that terror, then I would do it for her.

"Could you talk to us about Jewish notions of the afterlife?" I asked.

The rabbi seemed flustered, as if he'd never thought about this before, or had never been asked. He said that nobody knows what the afterlife is like, and that it is the Jewish tradition to think about immortality in terms of the children we bring into the world, and the people whose lives we've touched. "Gabbi," he said, turning to Beth, "will always have your eyes, or your chin, or smile. Her attitudes and values, the very sound of her voice, her expressions, in all kinds of ways, even beyond what she'll remember of you, will always bear your influence. So in that sense, your life will continue through her life, and through her children's lives. Where we actually go, what heaven is, or what it might mean to dwell there, well, we just don't know."

His answer was, of course, consistent with the values by which Beth had always lived, with that horizontal vision of transcendence that underlay her social activism. But didn't she need something more now, something that spoke directly to her soul, her actual being, where it would go, how it would continue, once her life was over? I thought about the prayers I'd read throughout my childhood at memorial services for relatives, or on the High Holidays: "O God full of compassion, Eternal Spirit of the universe, grant perfect rest under the wings of Your Presence to our loved one who has entered eternity. Master of Mercy, let her find refuge for ever in the shadow of your wings, and let her soul be bound up in the bond of eternal life. . . ." Why couldn't the rabbi have spoken to Beth about the hopefulness implicit in such prayers, about the consolation to be found there, the recompense for the sorrow and brevity and unfairness of what had befallen her? Beth didn't need careful distinctions, hedged arguments, qualification or uncertainty, or some sort of figurative afterlife. She needed reassurance of a literal one, she needed literal refuge. My goodness, there are 613 laws a Jew is required to obey in order to be a good Jew, and all the rabbi sees fit to offer by way of otherworldly reward for a virtuous life is memory! That's one hell of a small carrot for such a huge stick. As I listened to the rabbi, as I watched my sister watch him without expression, poker-faced, hiding, it seemed, what I imagined was a harrowing disappointment behind an unreadable impassivity, I felt flood through me all of my old anger at the hypocrisy and inadequacy and sheer irrelevance of institutional religion.

When he was finished, Beth asked if she could take a few books out of the library. He said No problem, do you have your card? No, she hadn't ever gotten a card. Well, the librarian was out on lunch break by now, but he could open up the library and let her take what books she wanted so long as she promised to return them. She took out several books on death and dying, and on Jewish mysticism. As we were leaving, the rabbi told her again to remember to return the books, though there was absolutely no rush. "Easy for you to say," Beth mumbled under her breath. "Well, kiddo," I told her when we were out of earshot of the rabbi, "there's one advantage to being terminally ill. What's he gonna do, sue you if you forget?" Beth put her hand up over her mouth to make sure the rabbi couldn't hear her giggling.

*   *   *   *

On Monday morning, the day before Beth was to be moved into the hospice, we had a visit from a hospital volunteer. Beth hadn't wanted anyone to see her since she'd been hospitalized the week before, mostly because she felt too ill for visitors. As I mentioned earlier, throughout the day she was either in terrible pain or half asleep in a morphine stupor. But she also knew that she looked awful, and didn't want anyone to see her in such a state. So Russ put the word out to her many friends and colleagues that no one should visit her until we got her to the hospice and her pain was more under control. From Saturday till Monday, we saw no one at all aside from nurses.

I was reading, Beth was dozing, when a perky middle-aged woman entered the room without knocking, and went right up to the bed. A Bible in one hand, she exuded radiant, even arrogant good health; full of her own benevolence, it seemed to me, she was hell-bent on solacing anyone in her path. Beth half-opened her eyes as the woman leaned over her and took her hands, and asked her, Are you afraid, dear? Before Beth could answer, the woman said, "It's okay to be afraid. I was afraid too when I was where you are, but I got better because I trusted in the Lord, and I know you can too."

Then she turned to me and asked, "And who are you? Her son?"

Beth shrugged her shoulders, and laughed almost apologetically, "He's my brother. It's been a hard couple of days."

"Of course it has," the woman answered, immune to irony.

Then leaning closer to my sister's face, squeezing her hands again, she said, "It's hard to believe that anyone really wins the lottery, but people do win it. They do win the lottery. I know because I won it once, and I can tell from looking in your eyes that you can win it too if you just believe. Just put your faith in Jesus, and you'll be home with your family in no time."

As soon as she left, I leaned over the bed, took my sister's hands in mine, and said in my most sincere voice, "What a crock."

Beth looked up toward the heavens. Barely above a whisper she began to half chant, half sing: "O Lord won't you buy me a Mercedes Benz, my friends all drive Porsches, I must make amends, worked hard all my lifetime, no help from my friends, O Lord won't you buy me a Mercedes Benz."

About an hour later, a small stout man arrived at the room, a Bible in his hand. "How are you doing?" he asked Beth. "Not bad," she said, opening her eyes a moment, then closing them again. "And who are you?" he asked me. "Her son?"

"Listen, pal," I said before Beth had a chance to correct him. "There was someone here an hour ago, and . . ."

"A good-lookin' gal 'bout my age?"

"Yeah," I said, "and . . ."

"That's my better half. Some little lady, huh!"

"Sure is. But if you don't mind we don't want any more visitors today. My sister's really tired."

"No need to explain," he boomed. "You all take care of yourselves. God bless."

"Yeah, sure, God bless."

I went to the nurses' station and asked them, please, to keep the evangelicals away from my sister's room. Then I called the rabbi to let him know that Beth's condition had taken a dramatic turn for the worse. "She really needs some consolation, Rabbi, and I was wondering if you could stop by today or tomorrow and talk with her. You know, about God and heaven." He said he'd be there in the morning.

*   *   *   *

*B*y that point, I myself needed the consolation, the reassurance, almost as much as Beth. Beth's lucidity was wavering and intermittent. It took more and more morphine to control the pain, which meant she spent more and more time asleep. And when she did wake she still talked about going to Michigan, about getting Gabbi's hair cut, about summer plans, and now I didn't try to contradict her. If she knew she was dying, she was still operating under the time frame she was given back in May—she thought she still had months to live, that death would happen sometime in the fall, and that her summer plans were still intact.

Luckily, she was awake when the rabbi arrived. He hadn't seen her since our meeting with him back in May. He was clearly very moved to see her, his face showing the shock of disbelief that must have shown on my face when I arrived on Friday.

Like the evangelical woman the day before, he asked Beth if she was scared, and she said, yes, she was. Then he said again he couldn't tell her what would happen to her when she died. Of course, her soul would return to God but what that meant, what possible mode of existence that would be, was unimaginable. What he could say with certainty was that everyone whose life Beth had touched would carry her with them as a blessing. Beth kept her eyes closed as he was speaking, and only opened them when he asked her how her family was taking the news. At this, she turned to me and asked, having again forgotten that she'd asked me this already a couple of days before, "Do Ma and Dad know?"

"Yes," I said. "I've already told them."

"How are they taking the news?"

"Well, you know, Beth, they're heartbroken but they're hanging in there."

"Are they coming here?"

"Yes, they'll be here this afternoon. They're on their way already."

"And David?" she asked. "Does he know?"

"Yes, I've told him too, and he'll be here in a couple of days."

"And what about Alan?"

"Alan?" I asked, not knowing what to say.

"Yes, Alan," she repeated. "Has he been told? Is he all right? Have you talked to him?" Before I could answer, she suddenly recognized me, she shook her head and laughed.

"Of course I've told Alan," I continued, since she was laughing now, the first time I'd seen her really laugh since I'd arrived, and I didn't want her to stop. "In fact, I talk to him every day. He and I, you know, we've grown quite close over the last few weeks. Whenever anything happens to me, he's always the first to know. And vice versa."

Before he left, the rabbi asked Beth if there was anything she wanted. And turning to me she said she wanted to laugh again, did I know a joke? I told the one about the Jewish American, the Mexican American, the African American, and the WASP who've died and gone to heaven. At the Pearly Gates, St. Peter tells them that since they've all lived exemplary lives, they will each be granted one wish for the world they've left behind. The Jewish American says he wishes all Jews could return to Israel so they could live among their own kind free of anti-Semitism. And St. Peter says, "Your wish is granted. You may enter heaven." The Mexican American says he wishes that all Mexican Americans could return to Mexico and live there in peace and prosperity in their own country, among their own people. St. Peter tells him, "Your wish is granted. You may enter heaven." The African American says he wishes that all African Americans could return to Africa and live without racism among their own kind as a free and equal people. "Your wish is granted," St. Peter says. "You may enter heaven." The WASP says, "Let me get this straight. All the Jews have gone back to Israel. All the Mexicans have gone back to Mexico. And all the blacks have gone back to Africa." "That's right," St. Peter answers. "Well in that case," the WASP replies, "I'll take a Diet Coke."

*   *   *   *

Later that morning, just before I was to leave for the airport to pick up my parents, and Beth herself was to be taken to the hospice, Russ came by with two letters. The first, addressed to Beth, was from the president of Rice University, informing her that she had been promoted to the position of vice provost. Beth laughed ruefully after Russ read it out. "So I'll be vice provost for a month. Big deal." The other letter was an official announcement from the sociology department, publicizing the establishment of the Beth Shapiro Award. "This award," the letter read, "will be presented at the University's Annual Awards Dinner to a graduating sociology major who, in the judgment of the department, has exhibited some of the special qualities of spirit or character that call to mind our colleague Beth Shapiro: courage, grace, perseverance in pursuit of a laudable goal, verve, empathy, love of life, humor, the ability to overcome challenges, concern for the underdog, moral strength, a sense of responsibility to loved ones and to society, and a winning personality."

Beth was moved to tears. "This is so wonderful," she said. "Now I'll be remembered in perpetuity." Whether or not the award had made her less afraid to die, it did appear to give her, for now at least, a sense of having lived a life that mattered, a sense too of some continuing existence that was consistent with the life she'd led. That's why she said the words "in perpetuity" with such conviction, such gratitude and pleasure. Maybe the rabbi was right in saying what he said to Beth. Maybe he knew what Beth was teaching me to see—that whatever consolation we may find as we approach our death will be the consolation that the lives we've led have readied us to find.

Russ held the letter up before her, and Beth gazed upon it as if it were the Book of Life itself.

*B*eth walked for the last time in her life two days after I arrived. "Al," she said, "I have to pee." When I moved to call the nurse, she held her hand up to stop me. "Don't bother. I can't wait. You take me."

I raised the bed. I pulled the covers back. My arm around her back, her hand on my shoulder for support, I carefully eased her down and walked her the four or five feet to the bathroom. I wanted to help her all the way to the toilet, not just to the bathroom door, but Beth insisted that I wait outside, she could get herself seated, she didn't need my help for that. Yesterday, however, she had slipped and fallen trying to sit down. The doctor advised her to use a bedpan, but, in the nurse's words, Beth wouldn't "cooperate." When I asked her about the bedpan, she replied, "I'd rather fall and kill myself than shit in bed."

Still clinging to what privacy and independence was left her, she held the guardrail with one hand while the other hand drew the door shut behind her.

Even as I marveled at her determination, I was shaken by her helplessness. Aside from the few years of her exile from the family when she and I had no contact, Beth brought an almost motherly passion to her role of older sister. She used to say that when I was a baby I belonged to her, and that all through my infancy and toddlerhood she protected me from baby-sitters who were insufficiently attentive to my needs, and from my brother's depredations—David, three years older than I, didn't gracefully relinquish his status as the only male child in the family.

Even later, in my late teens and early twenties, when we resumed our friendship, I was always her little brother. I discovered the depth and passion of that protectiveness in the summer between my freshman and sophomore years at college when I hitchhiked out to Michigan to visit her for the first time. My parents didn't want me to go—"What do you mean, hitchhiking?" Nor were they crazy about the idea of my consorting with Beth's radical friends. They were afraid that she'd politicize me—"brainwash" me was how my father put it.

I visited only for a few days, right before the start of school. It was a memorable trip. I was on my own, away from the parents, for practically the first time in my life. I was with Beth again after all those years, flattered by her attention toward me, her seemingly inexhaustible and non-judgmental interest in what I thought and who I was. A couple of times, Beth, her boyfriend Derry, and I even got high together, which I regarded as an almost sacramental gesture of intimacy and respect. I felt as if I'd found a new home with all the security that home entailed and none of the hassles.

On the night before I hitchhiked back to Boston, Beth took me to a local bar to meet a group of friends. Among them was a woman named Becky. She was twenty-four, about my sister's age. And very beautiful. Too shy to speak, I gawked at her all evening, careful to glance away whenever she'd look in my direction. She was seated next to a man who, I found out later, was her boyfriend. All night, the two of them seemed to ignore each other.

For a couple of hours or so, I drank and chatted with this or that person to whom Beth proudly introduced me. She was pleased at how easily I made myself at home in her world, in the life she'd made for herself here in Lansing. It gratified her that I fit in and held my own among her friends, that they all seemed to like me and that I liked them.

After a while, Becky announced that she was tired and asked me if I'd drive her home. I was surprised, to say the least. Beth too looked surprised, and a little suspicious.

"What do you say, Beth," I asked, "you mind if I give Becky a lift?"

"I guess I can catch a ride with someone else," she said. "Are you sure you know the way?"

"Come on, Beth," Becky laughed, "what are you, his mother? He's a big boy. He can take care of himself."

The whole way to her house, Becky didn't talk much, except to give directions. To my amazement, she asked me in, and before I knew what was happening we were in bed. The lovemaking was fast but probably not so furious, at least from her perspective—though to me it hardly mattered. I had fallen head over heels in love, and too mystified by my astounding good fortune to notice whether she was pleased or not, I assumed she loved me too. Almost as soon as we were finished, Becky said my sister would worry if I stayed too long. And anyway, since I was leaving early in the morning I'd probably want to get some sleep. I don't remember how I explained to myself her eagerness to get me out of her apartment, but explain it I did. And by the time I'd gotten back to Beth's, I'd convinced myself that Becky and I were meant to be together.

Beth was waiting up for me. I told her what had happened, that Becky and I had reached a kind of understanding. Beth didn't seem pleased at all. She didn't tell me I was utterly deluded, only that I shouldn't make too much of what had happened. She told me that the man next to Becky at the bar was her boyfriend. They'd been having trouble lately, and besides Becky wasn't the most reliable of people. "Just don't jump to any conclusions, Al," she said. "You don't know anything about her. Just think it over." The next morning, as she drove me to the highway where I'd begin the long hitch back to Boston, she repeated what she'd said the night before. The more she tried to talk me out of this infatuation, advising patience, reason, caution, the more she sounded like our mother. When I told her so, she said, "Okay, do what you want. Let's drop the subject." She was clearly stung by the comment.

As soon as I got home, I wrote Becky a love letter. I shudder to think what I must have sounded like. At the time, my favorite books were Lawrence Ferlinghetti's *A Coney Island of the Mind,* Kahlil Gibran's *The Prophet,* and Rod McKuen's *Listen to the Warm.* In a language that was undoubtedly more Pop than Beat or Buddhist, I squeezed every drop of sap out of my adolescent heart. All Becky had to do was say the word, and I'd drop out of school and move to Lansing.

By the time the letter reached her, Becky had made up with her boyfriend. Apparently, I was how she got him interested in her again. She never answered the letter. What happened next I heard a few weeks later—not from Beth but from Derry. On the phone with him, I was distraught because I hadn't heard from Becky. Did he think she'd gotten the letter? Did Becky say anything about me to him or Beth? Had they seen her? "Look, Al," Derry said, exasperated, "Beth told me not to say anything to you about this, but I don't know how else you're gonna come to your senses." Becky, he went on to say, had gotten my letter all right. In fact, she had found it so amusing that she brought it to the bar one night when Beth wasn't around. She read the letter to all their friends, and they all had a good laugh at my expense. He also told me that when word got back to Beth, she confronted Becky in the same bar in front of the same people. She dressed her down pretty thoroughly, called her a selfish no-good bitch. Bad enough that Becky had used me to get back at her boyfriend, but to ridicule me the way she had was unforgivable. Beth, he said, hadn't spoken to Becky since. Probably never would.

At the time, I was devastated, but as I got over Becky I also felt enormous gratitude for what Beth did—not only for having confronted Becky, but also for not telling me about it, for wanting to spare me any knowledge of the whole humiliating incident.

I thought about this story as I waited at the bathroom door. I thought about Beth's loyalty to me, how fierce and unconditional it was. I remembered how Beth used to tell me that she didn't think she'd ever marry or raise a family, or ever reconcile with Ma and Dad. In those days I was in effect her only family. And since I too at the time was on the outs with Ma and Dad, I turned to Beth (as she had to me) for the familial comforts that my parents couldn't give, it seemed, without stern judgment, accusation, disapproval. I thought about how much I owed her, how in my late teens and early twenties when I was always haplessly lovelorn, insecure, and diffident, I depended on her for advice and reassurance.

Now I wanted somehow to do for her what she had done for me. But there was nothing I could do. Struggling to pull herself up from the toilet seat, she finally had to call me in for help: there was no protection or defense against the disintegration of her dignity. All I could do was go to her and lift her from the seat, and hold her firmly enough so she could use her hands to keep her robe closed, her privacy momentarily intact, as we walked the five or six steps back across the room; all I could do was ease her down into the bed, and call the nurse, and though it wasn't time yet for another shot of morphine, argue with him till he finally gave in, and administered the shot, so Beth could sleep.

*I*n his prison diary, *Dialogue with Death,* Arthur Koestler describes how his physical, life-and-death dependence on his warders grew into a psychological and spiritual dependence over the course of his imprisonment, such that he came to think of them as "naturally" superior beings, and of himself as "naturally" inferior:

> I did not know how quickly one comes to regard a privileged stratum of men as beings of a higher biological species and to take their privileges for granted as though they were natural endowments. Don Ramon has the key and I am in the cage; Don Ramon as well as I look upon this state of things as entirely natural and are far from regarding it as in any way an anomaly. And if a crazy agitator were to come and preach to us that all men are equal, we should both laugh him to scorn; Don Ramon with all his heart, I, it is true, only half-heartedly—but all the same I should laugh.

What Koestler says here about the relation between prisoner and guard, the atavistic dependency one comes to feel toward those who have total power over one's existence, was true in a way of Beth's relationship with all her doctors, her oncologist especially. In the same way that for Koestler the "whole mood of a night or an afternoon [would depend] on the tone of voice of Angelito or the warder" when they'd bring him food ("I react to friendly or unfriendly waves like a seismograph"), my sister's moods, her hopes, her view of the world, understandably depended not only on her doctor's findings but on the doctor's tone of voice, his every gesture. Reduced by her disease to almost infantile helplessness, she came to see her doctor as an all-knowing and all-powerful parent. Since her survival depended on his expertise, it was impossible for her not to invest that expertise with almost magical potency.

But in the course of that unavoidable projection of authority, something peculiar happened. Dr. P. became not just her potential savior but also her potential judge. More than anyone else, early and late in her disease, he determined how she felt about herself. When she was doing well, meaning when she responded well to the treatment he prescribed, he bolstered her self-esteem by saying he was proud of her, she was his best patient, she was his favorite patient. But if he were the benevolent deity when she was doing well, responding to his treatment, he became the *deus absconditus* when the cancer had metastasized, and it was clear that she was going to die. Her status as patient may have changed, but her emotional attachment to her doctor hadn't. If anything, in the final stages of her illness, her need for his human empathy, his care, his interest in her, if not for his encouragement, was stronger than ever at the very point when he had disappeared. In her last days in the hospital, and even after she had moved into the hospice, over and over Beth would ask for Dr. P. She'd continue saying that Dr. P. didn't like her anymore, that he didn't want to see her, that she had obviously let him down. In Beth's mind pleasing her oncologist and getting well had become one and the same thing.

Beth of course by then had been infantilized by the tumor

in her brain, as well as by massive amounts of morphine. But it wasn't just the drugs and the disease that made her feel somehow responsible for failing to get better, that made her feel unworthy of the treatment her doctor, in all his wisdom, had provided. That dependency and helplessness were also encouraged, I think, partly by the chronic combination of high-tech treatments and hyperspecialized language: the repeated bone scans and MRIs that told nothing and everything, the hours she'd spent in waiting rooms, bored, anxious, anticipating two minutes of a doctor's attention, the feeling that her body was inseparable from the plastic tubes and monitors without which she couldn't live, not to mention the bewildering complexities of navigating the exclusions of her insurance coverage. Everything about her treatment undermined her sense of agency and power. In falling ill, Beth came to feel that she was serving the needs and interests of the medical profession, not being served by them.

On top of all her mortal grief and terror, Beth toward the end of her life also felt a wholly artificial and unjustified sense of guilt about her body and her illness. However much that guilt was a symptom of her disintegrating mind, it was also an emotional reflection or effect of the treatment she'd received, the emotional equivalent of the category into which she had been put when she had gone beyond the reach of cure or palliation. On her medical record she officially became a treatment failure—not someone whom the treatment failed, but someone who had failed the treatment.

*   *   *   *

About two weeks after we had moved into the hospice, I awoke to find Dr. P. standing by Beth's bed. It was a little after seven in the morning. I have no idea how long he'd been standing there. In silence, he was looking down at

Beth, his expression grim but controlled. Beth was awake. She was looking up at him, waiting for him to speak, it seemed. After a while, he said, "Let's see what they have you on." And he pulled out from beneath her pillow the automative syringe driver, or morphine pump, the thread-thin IV tube running from it to her shoulder. "Uh-huh," he said, "very good." Then he checked her chart and after another moment said, "So." Then more silence. Then his beeper went off. He glanced at it, said he had to go, but that he'd be back soon in a day or so to see how she was doing. He never so much as looked at me as he walked out. That was the last time we would see him.

All the same, I was glad that he had come. I was glad to see him standing there uncomfortably, fumbling with emotions that squared so awkwardly with his professionalism. Dr. P. was an excellent doctor. Most of Beth's physicians were. I have no doubt that the medical attention he gave my sister was beyond reproach. As I watched him hem and haw ineptly at my sister's bedside, I wondered about his other patients. How many did he have? How many of them at the moment were dying like Beth, or soon to be dying? Of course it would have been impossible for him to reciprocate their feelings, to attach himself emotionally to each of them as they had no doubt attached themselves to him. To survive in that particular subspecialty, to provide his patients with the best possible care, some measure of detachment would of course be necessary. At the same time, didn't he owe his patients what he or the nature of his profession had encouraged them to desire and expect? If, while they responded to his treatment, he was going to allow his patients to perceive him as a god, hero, or omnipotent parent dispensing praise and hope and self-esteem, didn't his obligations toward them as a fellow human being, as someone with whom they'd been intimately involved for months or years, continue even after, as a doctor, there was nothing else that he could do?

Why hadn't he returned any of Russ's calls two weeks ago when Beth was hospitalized? And yet it took him less than thirty seconds to return a call from Bill Redwine, a fellow doctor, when he called on our behalf. That fact almost more than any other typified for me a skewed allegiance, that the doctor placed his obligation to his colleagues, and to the medical profession itself, above his obligation to his patient and to his patient's family. Why didn't he wait till we were there with Beth before he broke the news to her that she had only days or weeks to live? And why did he prescribe that last dose of chemotherapy that, according to Bill Redwine, would only sicken the tumors on the lining of her brain but not kill them? Did that last treatment extend her life? By how much, a day or two? In doing so, it also ravaged her mouth and throat with sores, so that she paid for those potential extra days with extra suffering.

In *How We Die,* Sherwin Nuland describes the way oncologists and subspecialists in general are conditioned by their training as well as temperament to perceive their patients as problems to be solved, as riddles to be mastered, more than as people to be cared for. According to Nuland, oncologists are driven by a preternatural fear of death. Each patient they bring back from the brink of extinction seems to confirm their own invulnerability. Those patients, on the other hand, who "fail them" dramatize the limits of their power, the frailty of their illusion of immunity from death, which their professionalism helps them to sustain. Not to withdraw from their patients when they become a riddle that will not be solved is to confront their own mortality. Even more than the fear of lawsuits, it is the fear of death that compels the doctor to prolong life, at almost any cost, even after there's no hope of victory, even when, as in Beth's case, the prolongation only means more suffering and pain.

*   *   *   *

After Beth died, and I returned home to my family in Chapel Hill, I received hundreds of condolence cards and letters from friends and acquaintances around the country. I was surprised at how much consolation I received from even the most cursory expressions of sympathy. Oddly enough, almost the only person I did not hear from was my wife's brother, a neuro-ophthalmologist who lives in a nearby town. After several weeks passed, I wrote my brother-in-law expressing how hurt and disappointed I was by his failure so much as to acknowledge my sister's death. He didn't answer my letter. When my wife called to ask him why, he first said, "What letter?" pretending he hadn't read it, then he went on to say that he had glanced at it and since he saw that it had to do with an uncomfortable subject, he put it aside. When she pressed him to elaborate, he said that he could see that the letter expressed what he called "a dysfunctional response to the death of someone he didn't know," and he didn't feel at all obliged to answer. Eventually, he did respond, coldly but dutifully, after a good deal of pressure from his parents.

Now I should add that my brother-in-law is an excellent doctor, one of the top neuro-ophthalmologists in the country. A teaching physician at a prestigious university hospital, he's renowned for spending hours upon hours with his patients, and for ignoring the hospital administration's demands that he work in a more cost-efficient manner, that he generate more revenue by herding more patients in and out of his office in a given day. He refuses to compromise the rigorous standards of his professionalism in the name of money.

I wonder, though, if there isn't a connection between his indisputable excellence as a doctor and his "discomfort" with the sort of feelings I demanded from him, between the rigorous standards by which he's lived the better part of his existence and his assumption that any expression of feeling beyond the bounds of what his discipline demands must be "dysfunctional." The biomedical nature of the word "dysfunction" is itself a reflection of his hyperspecialized view of life, of his tendency to view even nonmedical experience through the narrow lens of his expertise.

"It's not that he doesn't feel anything," my father-in-law explained, trying to appease me. "It's that he feels too much, he just doesn't know how to show it." Initially, I dismissed this argument, still too aggrieved by his failure to show even a modicum of sympathy for me or for my family. But now as I think about how Dr. P. stood paralyzed with awkwardness by my sister's bedside, I wonder if my father-in-law isn't right, to some extent. Dr. P. and my brother-in-law are products of the hyperspecialized culture of medicine, a culture within which they have spent most of the waking hours of their adult life, and a good part of their adolescence. Within the margins of their role as problem-solver, as biomedical guru, they feel what their profession enables them to feel; they're even comfortable with feelings like compassion so long as it's a doctor's compassion, the compassion of someone in control, of someone still effectual, of someone with a problem that's still capable of being solved.

It could be, as I suspected at the time, that my brother-in-law just didn't feel enough to write me when I returned from Houston. And it could be that Dr. P. was simply awkward in the face of someone whom he couldn't help. But what I now choose to think is that they both were capable of feeling, but were incapable of knowing what to do with how they felt. Though it seemed he struggled to maintain his superior role as doctor at my sister's bedside—checking the morphine pump, examining her chart—her status as a treatment failure forced him to face her not as a doctor but as a needy, fearful, fellow human being, as just another mortal citizen among the dying. She was asking him, as I had asked my brother-in-law, to speak a language that he couldn't master.

A few days after Beth was moved into the hospice, my brother arrived from Pittsburgh, where he was doing a summer stock production of the musical *Cabaret*. That whole week, Beth's condition was uncertain. She'd passed very little water, and she'd been having fits of what the nurses called terminal fever and terminal restlessness. They predicted that death could come any day now, though they were quick to remind us that the end of life is as mysterious as the beginning of life, and if the dying had any unfinished business, if there was someone they wanted to see, or some event they wanted to attend, or hear about, they could hold on for many days, even weeks. Maybe, one nurse told me in the middle of the night when Beth was especially agitated, maybe she's waiting to die until your brother gets here.

Not likely, I thought, since she and David were never close. From earliest childhood their relations were always barbed with competitiveness and animosity. Beth, the eldest child, resented the attentions that David, as the first male child, received. She also resented the fanfare his musical talents elicited from everyone in the family, especially from our mother, who spent most weekends squiring David to his various lessons, rehearsals, and engagements. He began performing professionally when he was five years old. David, in turn, felt intimidated by Beth's intellectual gifts. While Beth always excelled in school, schoolwork for David was a trial, and the better Beth got at her studies, the more David concentrated all of his efforts on his budding show-business career, on what secured his status in the family.

As the "baby" in the family, I got along well enough with both of them. I was always perhaps a little closer to my sister, partly because I was farther away from her in age, and partly because we shared a passion for basketball and football (David, too busy with show business, was never much of a sports fan). Also, later in life, as university professors, Beth and I shared a love of books, and whenever the three of us were together David often felt intimidated and excluded by our intellectual interests. Throughout our childhood, David and I had our squabbles, certainly, but they were never as frequent or intense as his and Beth's. As I grew older, I often found myself cast in the role of mediator and go-between, passing messages along from one sibling to the other when they themselves weren't talking. While I have memories of playing happily with either one of them, I have no memory of the three of us ever doing anything together, aside from watching television on the weekends.

Their relations, never good, hit bottom on a Friday night in 1965 when Beth, a sophomore at MSU and home on break, was given use of the family car to visit friends. She had gone out early, before dinner. While the rest of us were eating, David asked if he could use the car that night. My father told him he was too late, that he'd already given the car to Beth, and she was gone for the evening.

"Why does she get the car whenever she wants it?"

"She doesn't always get the car," Dad said.

"But I have plans, too," David whined. "My friends need me to drive."

"Hey," my father shot back, "don't take that tone with me. Your sister's only home for a few days."

"Fine," David yelled; he was standing now. "Fine. Give her the car. Let her go see her nigger friends."

"What did you say? What are you talking about?" Ma asked.

"You want to know, go ask her yourself." And he stormed out.

I already knew about Beth's black boyfriend. The day she got home, she pulled me aside and showed me a picture of him. She asked me what I thought. I thought he had some tan. She hugged me and made me promise not to breathe a word to Ma and Dad. She must have showed David the picture too. Bad as their relationship always was, she must have still assumed that he would not betray her. Maybe she even needed his approval, as she needed mine, in order to lessen her fearful isolation from the family, which her secret romance with a forbidden black man must have made her feel. I don't know.

I never got a chance to ask her. My father went up to Beth's room. He found her diary and broke it open, and what he read must have confirmed my brother's accusation. What I remember next are phone calls to wherever it was my sister had gone that night, my mother crying, my father screaming into the phone that Beth had shamed her parents, that she was no longer a member of the family, she was nothing but a slut, a trollop, she should come and get her things and never come back. Later that night, Beth arrived with the father of a friend of hers, an Episcopal minister, who tried unsuccessfully to mediate, or if not mediate, then protect Beth from my father's wrath. David and I had crept halfway down the stairs. We couldn't see anyone, but we could hear each word of the fight, which lasted hours, the shouting and the sobs. Finally we heard Beth yell that Dad had no right to read her diary, and she could do whatever the hell she wanted. Then we heard a loud slap. Beth was crying as she ran from the house. From my bedroom window, I could see her on the sidewalk across the street, under the streetlamp. She was holding her face in both hands, her shoulders heaving as the minister, his arm around her, helped her into the car, and then the two of them drove away.

I was too stunned by the violence to wonder at the time what David must have felt as he sat beside me on the stairs and listened to what his outburst had set in motion. Was he horrified at what he'd done? Did he feel ashamed for having squealed on Beth, and over something so petty? Or did he feel in some way vindicated, having finally proven to my parents that he was the worthier child? Or did he feel at once ashamed and vindicated? We never talked about what happened, or how he felt about it. And from then on, Beth was never mentioned in the house.

As far as my father was concerned, he didn't have a daughter. We, my brother and I, were not to write or call her.

I was thirteen at the time, old enough to understand what happened, and secretly to take my sister's side, but too young, too dependent on and fearful of my parents to speak up for Beth. I hated them for what they did to her, my mother especially. While she didn't approve of Beth's involvement with a black man, she wasn't as virulently racist as my father. Yet she refused to fight him. Caught between the claims of wife and mother, she had taken sides and gone along with his decision to disown their daughter. Rightly or wrongly, I held her more responsible than my father for my sister's pain, and for the pain her absence caused me. If there's one thing a mother is supposed to do, it's to protect her children from harm. And if she'd stand by while her husband threw her daughter out, wouldn't she do the same thing when it was my turn to fight my father for my independence? On the other hand, I didn't stand up for Beth either. And maybe my mother was just an easier target for my anger because I identified with her, because I could hear my cowardly silence in her own. Only years later did my mother tell me that throughout this period she indirectly kept in touch with Beth behind my father's back. She regularly called Beth's friends, her teachers, even her therapist, to see how she was doing. She even sent her money from time to time. Now when I imagine the pain she must have felt—having to abandon her daughter as she herself had been abandoned (although for different reasons)—I'm ashamed of having judged her as harshly as I did back then.

Like my mother, I too kept faith with Beth, however feebly. Through Beth, I'd acquired a love of soul music. And in the months and years that followed her disownment, I bought many of the albums that I knew she liked: the Four Tops' greatest hits, the Temptations' greatest hits, albums by Aretha Franklin, Otis Redding, Marvin Gaye. My father hated Motown and soul music. It reminded him of Beth and of her love life. One day he caught me playing these records. He stormed into my room, gathered the records up, and dumped them in the garbage. He didn't want any *shvartzer* music in his house, he yelled. From then on, I hid the records from him, playing them only when he wasn't home. My small symbolic declaration of allegiance with my banished sister.

It wasn't until I went away to college that Beth and I resumed our friendship. Eventually, my parents reestablished a relationship with her, though it was never very good. On their side there was more than a residual disapproval and even shame over Beth's boyfriends, who were mostly black, and never Jewish, a disapproval and shame that their pride in her accomplishments could never quite offset. On Beth's side, she could never get over the pain of having been abandoned by her parents, could never quite forgive them for that pain. Nor did she ever quite forgive David. They too got back in touch eventually. From time to time Beth would go to New York to see David in whatever show he might be doing. And once or twice he even visited her in Michigan. But they were never friends. So far as I know, Beth never again entrusted David with any intimate details about her life.

*　　*　　*　　*

David called every day that week. The show in Pittsburgh was closing on Friday. And when Beth was well enough to talk, he'd ask her please to hold on until he got there. Beth would mumble that she wasn't going anywhere, which David took to mean that she would wait to die until he had a chance to say goodbye to her in person.

Then he was here. He entered the room and still several feet from the bed he leaned over sideways, so that his face was level with Beth's face as he approached. He duck-walked that way over to her bed, looking theatrical and ludicrous all at once. At the bedside, he kneeled down, one hand holding the guardrail. "Hey, Beth," he said, and kissed her. Beth, too weak to talk, smiled faintly, and then just looked at him. David seemed as if he were about to cry, and then he noticed that my mother was drinking Evian water. "Hey," he said, "have you ever noticed that Evian spelled backwards is Naive? Think about it." He was looking at Beth but really talking to the rest of us. Now he was saying that he had a great joke for us all, a joke one member of the *Cabaret* cast had told him. "You won't believe it, it's one of the funniest things I've ever heard, but you got to hear this guy tell it, it's all in the timing. I made a tape of it, I've got it with me." And noticing the tape player on the other side of the bed, he went over to it, pulled the cassette tape from his briefcase and slipped it into the machine.

"Okay, now everybody quiet, you got to listen to this carefully."

The voice on the tape spoke a mile a minute, like an auctioneer:

"Story about a teacher getting acquainted with her kids the first day of school around the second grade.

"She says to the first little boy, What's your name?

"He says, Barnum Bailey.

"She says, How do you spell it?

"He says, B.A.R.N.U.M. B.A.I.L.E.Y.

"She says, NO! You should take it by syllables.

"She says, B.A.R., there's your BAR,

"N.U.M., there's your NUM,

"there's your BARNUM.

"B.A.I., there's your BAI,

"there's your NUM BAI,

"there's your BARNUM BAI

"L.E.Y., there's your LEY,

"there's your BAILEY,

"there's your NUM BAILEY,

"there's your BARNUM BAILEY.

"She says to the next little kid, What's your name?

"He says Archibald S. Holcomb.

"She says, How do you spell it?

"He says, Do you want me to spell it like you did with that kid's name?

"She says, Yes.

"He says, A.R.C.H., there's your ARCH

"I., there's your I.,

"there's your ARCH I.,

"B.A.L.D., there's your BALD,

"there's your I-BALD,

"there's your ARCHIBALD.

"S., there's your S., is your BALD-ass,

"is your I-BALD-ass,

"is your ARCHIBALD-ass,
"H.O.L. is your HOL,
"is your ass-HOL,
"is your BALD-ass-HOL,
"is your I-BALD-ass-HOL,
"is your ARCHIBALD-ass-HOL
"C.O.M.B. is your COMB,
"is your HOL-COMBed,
"is your ass-HOL-COMBed,
"is your BALD-ass-HOL-COMBed,
"is your I-BALD-ass-HOL-COMBed,
"is your ARCHIBALD S. HOLCOMB."

All of us, even Beth it seemed, were happy David had arrived. I described in the opening chapter how strange our usual interests and preoccupations had come to seem to us as we pursued them in the context of Beth's dying, that we were so self-conscious about the things we normally did that we in effect became performers of our own lives. Because of this, David, the professional performer, who was almost never not "on stage," paradoxically now seemed the least self-conscious of us all, the one most capable of putting us all at ease. He was a whirlwind of distraction, and distraction was what we sorely needed. My mother, ever the stage mom, loved hearing about the show he'd just finished, and what it would be like returning in a few days to the cast of *Sunset Boulevard,* from which he'd taken a two-month sabbatical so he could do the show in Pittsburgh. He'd also spend hours with her doing crossword puzzles. With my father, he talked golf and stocks. He went walking with him. He was constantly doing one or another of his many fine impressions: Frankie Fontaine's Crazy Guggenheim, Sammy Davis, Jr., Curly from the Three Stooges. His conversation in general was peppered with vaudeville lines and jokes. If anybody made some innocuous remark, like "Gee, it's so steamy today," David would shoot back in his Groucho Marx voice, "That's what she said at the picnic."

As always, he was the center of attention, but I was grateful to him now for taking center stage. I now had someone with whom to share the burden of the daily chores: someone else to run out each day for meals, and, when Russ couldn't, to take Gabbi to and from horseback-riding camp, to and from home to visit Beth; someone else to squire Ma and Dad back and forth between the hotel and the hospice, and to entertain them, help keep their spirits up. No one could make my parents laugh as David could. He also moved into the hospice with me, so I felt less alone at night, less solely responsible for Beth in the early morning hours. By doing all these things he made it easier for me and Ma to concentrate our energies on Beth.

David himself, though, seemed uncomfortable with Beth. She was largely out of it by then, either too tired, or too much in pain, or too disoriented from the morphine, to respond to any of his jokes. By then, too, our way of being with Beth was through touch mostly, not talk. When she'd get agitated or restless, or when her headaches would come on, and before the nurse would give her a boost of morphine, one of us, meaning my mother or me, would massage her neck and shoulders and her forehead until she fell asleep. David never volunteered to do this.

I knew he wanted desperately to reconnect with Beth, to convey to her the depth and intensity of his love and sorrow, and perhaps to make amends for what he'd done to her so many years ago. Shtick, however, was his most reliable way of being in the world, of relating to others. Like all of us in the family, David was never one for physical demonstrations of affection. But unlike me and Beth, he was never one for intimate conversations, either. His usual response to personal problems, his own or someone else's, was to shrug and say something dismissive, or innocuous, like "It is what it is," or "Just make the best of it." I think other people interpreted that dismissive shrug as saying that he couldn't be bothered, but what I think it really means is "I don't know how."

Like Dr. P., David is a specialist of sorts. After all, he's been in show business for more than forty years. The better part of all his waking hours had been spent mastering the techniques of musical comedy, learning to project his voice, learning how to block, to sing and dance, how not to overact. He was easiest, most himself, on stage. He too, I think, like Dr. P., was constrained by what he'd learned to do too well, by the discipline to which his whole life had been devoted. And while that discipline enabled him to perfect and master the sorts of feelings or expressions of feeling appropriate to the stage, it left him, when he was not on stage, like an actor who'd forgotten his lines. I've often thought that David would be more comfortable, in times of trouble, breaking into song than talking, since singing, for him, has come to be the most intimate place of feeling, the place where feeling disappears into the voice he's spent a lifetime learning to control.

One night, shortly after he arrived, I was massaging Beth's forehead, standing behind her bed. David had the tape recorder in his lap. He was transcribing the joke onto a yellow legal pad, so he could memorize it by the time he returned to New York. He couldn't wait to tell it to his friends in the *Sunset* cast, but he had to get the timing right. He'd play a second or two of the joke, then stop the tape, write down what he heard, then play another second or two. This went on for hours into the night. I had my eyes closed as I worked on Beth, half dreaming to the "B.A.I., there's your BAI," then silence, then "There's your NUM BAI," then more silence. At one point, I noticed that the silence went on longer than usual. My fingers gently moving in half circles across Beth's forehead, I looked up and caught David staring at me, at me and Beth. At that moment he seemed incredibly sad. I was just about to ask him if he wanted to spell me, and massage Beth for a while, when he turned the machine back on and listened with his finger on the stop button as the taped played "There's your BARNUM BAI. . . ." Then he pressed stop again and carefully wrote down what he heard.

*I*f it weren't for the tie that had no knot in it, the defense witness would have seemed the consummate professional in dress as well as manner. Under intense cross-examination from Marcia Clarke, he never lost his cool. Calmly, methodically, patiently, he defended his credentials, his various degrees and honors, his track record as director of a nationally renowned forensic crime lab, and even when Clarke got him to admit that being chairman of the chemistry department at Alfred University wasn't quite the distinction he made it out to be, since he was himself the only member of the department, he looked, spoke, and acted like the even-tempered expert that he was. His neatly trimmed beard, his tweedy sport coat, the starched white shirt all exuded straight-arrow conventionality, nononsense competence, a self-effacing pure disinterested concern for truth. Except for the tie. The tie hung from the inconspicuous collar as one long continuous strip of fabric down the front of his inconspicuous shirt. That he could sit there on national television in the trial of the century, answering questions as if there were nothing at all unusual in his appearance, as if his tie were knotted, made his apparent normalcy seem brazen and arrogant. Oddly enough, none of the TV commentators appeared to notice this.

What was his point? we wondered, my brother and I.

Was it a cult thing? Did the knotless tie signify membership in some secret society of criminologists? Or was it an otherwise conventional man's rebellion against the constraints of convention? His one small protest against societal norms, or some expression of solidarity—with whom? Or what? The tie equivalent of the yellow ribbon? And why didn't Marcia Clarke seize on this peculiarity and use it to impeach his testimony? Granted, the knotless tie would have fallen outside the scope of the examination, but couldn't she have indirectly, subliminally called attention to it and thereby undermined the doctor's credibility?

We turned the sound off. My brother took the role of Marcia Clarke, I took the role of Dr. MacDonald.

"Dr. MacDonald, you look awfully fit for a man your age. Do you work out at all?"

"Why yes I do at my local fitness center."

"And could you tell the jurors what sort of regimen you follow?"

"Well, I use a variety of Nautilus machines."

"Did you say *knotless* machines? *Knotless* like your tie, sir?"

"Excuse me?"

"Just answer the question. I remind you, you're under oath."

"Objection, your honor," my mother said from across the room where she was reading, "Ms. Clarke is badgering the witness."

"Overruled," my father muttered. "Proceed."

"Dr. MacDonald, if O. J. Simpson had committed these murders at sea, and fled from the scene in a motorboat but had to travel roughly the same distance between Bundy and Rockingham, how fast would he have to go in order to get home in time to meet the limo?"

"My best estimate would be five or six knots?"

"And you're familiar, are you *not,* sir, with *The Andy Griffith Show.*"

"Yes, I am."

"And can you tell the ladies and gentlemen of this jury the deputy's name on that show?"

"If my memory serves me well, I think his name was Barney."

"And what was Barney's real name?"

"Uh, Don something or other. . . ."

"Knotts, isn't that right, sir. Don Knotts!"

"Yes, that's it."

"No further questions."

We turned the sound back on. After a few moments my mother said, "How can you watch that crap all day? The whole thing's disgusting, especially Marcia Clarke."

"Marcia? What's wrong with Marcia?" my father asked. "I love Marcia."

"Oh, she's such a phony."

"Unlike Johnny Cochran," I sneered.

"He'd fuck a snake if he could get down low enough," my father added.

"I have to say, Ma, you seem a little too eager to cast aspersions on the prosecution team."

"I don't know what you're talking about."

"Strong women threaten you, don't they."

"Don't be silly."

"Women like Marcia Clarke."

"Come on."

"Like Nicole Brown Simpson."

"So what's your point?"

"My point is you don't live so far from Brentwood, do you? Where were you exactly on the night of June the twelfth?"

"Probably cleaning up after your father."

"Hey, don't drag me into this," my father said. "I don't remember where you were that night."

"You can't remember to put the seat up when you pee, so what does that prove?"

"Seems to me," I continued, "you could drive an ocean liner through your window of opportunity."

She waved me away with mock disgust. I could tell that she was done with joking. My brother David and I could draw her into our routines for a while, but sooner or later, usually sooner, the fact of where we were and what was happening to Beth would suddenly come back to her, her sorrow more intense for having been momentarily forgotten. Looking down at her book, she offered one last comment: "The police, the coroner, the prosecution, they all screwed up, and that's why Simpson's gonna walk." That was her usual refrain about the trial. The trial was a farce because the powers that be had proved to be incompetent or corrupt. If the authorities had only done their job, things would have been different. My father on the other hand was much more fatalistic. Like my mother, he was sure that Simpson had committed murder, but he also believed that no matter how well the evidence had been presented, and how aboveboard the authorities had acted, Simpson would still be acquitted, and not only or even primarily because he was a rich, famous, likable black man and his lawyers were pandering to a predominantly black jury, but because the world was by nature unjust, unfair, and because, in any situation, the worst eventuality was always the most likely thing to happen.

Except between the hours of one and three when my mother would watch her soaps, we had the trial on almost continually. Whether we watched or not, we liked to have it on. The court proceedings had become our Muzak, our white noise, the reliable fodder for the joking that David and I kept up for our parents' benefit, and for our own, too, in order to distract ourselves from the oppressive gloom. But the trial was more than just a refuge from my sister's illness. It was also a way for each of us obliquely to express our attitudes about what Beth was going through.

We could argue and obsess about the O. J. Simpson trial in part because we couldn't afford emotionally to argue and obsess about my sister, how or in what ways her illness and impending death were challenging our faith in life. The trial enabled us to turn away from what was painfully before us and at the same time indirectly articulate what each of us was feeling.

On the few occasions when we talked explicitly and in detail about my sister's cancer, my mother would fixate on the doctors and their incompetence in the same way that she would fixate on the incompetence of the prosecution team. Never mind that Beth's particular cancer has the lowest survival rate, that it's the fastest-growing kind there is, that the cells are so small that five or six billion of them have to mass together before even so much as a speck can be detected on an MRI, and that, despite two years of aggressive and debilitating treatment, Beth was never in remission and according to her doctors was lucky to live as long as she did. Still, my mother couldn't mention Beth's disease without repeating that her primary care physician had misread her mammogram, that the doctors were outrageously slow in detecting the metastasized tumor, that they'd mistaken her terrible headaches in the spring for sinus infections, her listlessness for acute depression. By training her anger on the doctors, she could put a human face on the disease. She could think that the disease, if not avoidable, could have been controlled. Implicit in her need to scapegoat someone for her daughter's illness was the refusal to acknowledge unintelligible pain, blameless suffering, a refusal born of a ferocious, admirable, and maddening insistence that life is good, no matter what, that happiness is possible, if not now, then later, if not here, then somewhere else.

Beth was betrayed by her doctors, just as the families of Nicole Brown and Ronald Goldman were being betrayed by incompetent attorneys, just as my mother herself had often felt betrayed, throughout her life, by a selfish husband, by aunts and uncles who were always much less attentive to her than she'd been to them, by children who have never perfectly conformed to her ideal of filial devotion. Despite a life beset with disappointment, so long as she could think her troubles had been caused by someone else's moral failure, inadvertent error, or momentary lapse, she could go on thinking trouble was avoidable. Once it was hedged about this way with explanation, with intelligible blame, trouble paradoxically confirmed the very optimism that it seemed to challenge. The more her circumstances contradicted her belief in happiness, the more she clung to that belief. And clinging to it in the teeth of trouble enabled her to weather even the most difficult of times.

But no trouble was ever like this trouble, no other time as difficult. Imagining the unimaginable—what it would be like to see one of my own children die—I can't help but think that the suffering my mother felt on Beth's behalf made all attempts at explanation futile, empty, hollow, even as it intensified her need to keep explaining, to scapegoat, to point the finger. More by habit than conviction, she would blame the doctors and then change the subject. After a while, she avoided the subject altogether. After a while, even her condemnations of the L.A.P.D. and the district attorney's office stopped.

My father dealt with Beth's illness the way he dealt with everything—by thinking there was nothing he or anyone could do about it. From the moment she was diagnosed with cancer, he went into mourning. In a sense, he's been in mourning his entire life—because he was the second son in a traditional Jewish family and therefore always came in second in his father's eyes; because Amos, the older brother, who was selfish, lazy, and unreliable, was nonetheless made a partner in the slaughterhouse while my father, despite his diligence and knack for business, was kept on as a salaried employee; because the war broke out and my father who'd enlisted in the army thereby lost a golden opportunity to prove himself the worthy son, for when my grandfather was caught selling meat on the black market, Amos, the diabetic, exempt from service, took the rap for him, and went to prison for a year, making the old man even more devoted to him. So once the war was over he demanded that my father go to work for Amos, which my father did, of course, even though by then he had ambitions to start a business of his own.

If it angered him, always to be the runner-up in the contest for his father's love, never to get his just reward, he learned with each new disappointment to assume that what he hadn't won he couldn't possibly have deserved. The less he received, the more dedicated to his father he became, the more compelled he was to say, as he always does, even now whenever he tells these stories, "My father always had my best interests at heart. He knew better than I did what I needed." If he blames anything, he blames his bad luck on having been born second, he blames "the cards you're dealt."

Beth's illness then was only the most recent and devastating instance of his never having gotten a fair shake. He could no more change or alleviate the pain he felt for his daughter than he could undo the macular degeneration in his left eye, or his Parkinson's syndrome, or his position in his family as the younger boy. When his sister, Hazel, died last year in her mid-eighties, he didn't talk about the good life she had, how happy her fifty years had been with her husband Joe, the many grandchildren and great-grandchildren they had fostered, the luxuries she lived among. He said, "Your life is over and they stick you in a box." He said it just as surely, with the same sad shrug of resignation, as he'd say that O. J., guilty as sin, was gonna walk.

My brother and I fell somewhere in between my mother's embittered optimism and my father's resigned fatalism. Like my mother, we blamed the doctors for screwing up so often, and like my father we believed Beth's chances of survival were never good, no matter what the treatment. Our anger toward the doctors was not unlike our anger toward the racist cop, the bungling coroner, the hapless criminologists, and the attorneys who had prepared their witnesses so poorly. And our fatalism with respect to Beth was also similar to our growing sense that a hung jury, at best, an acquittal at worst, would be inevitable.

And yet for me, the trial was connected to my sister in another way as well. A year ago when Beth had her stem cell transplant, she and I watched every moment of the preliminary hearings during the two weeks of her isolation. Beth had no interest in the trial per se. As an interracial couple, she and Russ were mostly amused by all the fuss and bother it provoked. They had no opinion as to Simpson's guilt or innocence, though from their own experience they could well believe a few rogue cops could frame a black man, especially one married to a blond-haired white woman. Nonetheless, all through her isolation, at least while I was visiting, she liked to watch the trial because of all the jokes we'd make about it. The laughter gave her some relief, however momentary, from the devastating effects of chemotherapy. And so in May, too, on my previous trip to Houston, the day after Beth's inoperable brain tumor was discovered, I was not surprised to find the trial flickering on the overhead television when I came into her room at Methodist Hospital. "We'll have to stop meeting like this," I said as I bent down to kiss her. And she replied, "I can't believe the O. J. Simpson trial is going to outlive me."

"Don't worry, Beth," I tried consoling her. "It's going to outlive us all." And now here we were in the middle of July, with my sister dying and the trial still going strong. By then the trial had become a kind of comfort, like an old friend in a foreign country, or some reliable marker in a landscape that was growing stranger and more frightening by the moment. But it was even more than this. My helplessness to save my sister's life awakened in me the magic thinking of a child. On some deep level, I believed Beth's life depended on the trial, that she would go on living so long as the trial continued, so long as we could joke about it. Like the grandfather clock whose ticking prolongs the old man's life in the song my children love to hear me sing ("Eighty years without slumbering, tick tock, tick tock, his life's seconds numbering, tick tock, tick tock, till the clock stopped, never to go again, and the old man died"), the trial, I'd come to believe, was keeping Beth alive.

*　　*　　*　　*

At one o'clock, my mother said, "It's time for my stories." She switched on *Days of Our Lives*. John had gone down to the city morgue to see the body of his wife, Marlena, one last time. For months, my mother informed us, Marlena had been acting strangely. A normally sweet and considerate woman, she suddenly started acting like a shrew, a harridan, for periods of time, her usual kindness alternating unpredictably with fits of unprovoked rage and cruelty. What John, her children, her colleagues at work, didn't know was that the Devil had been weaseling his way into her soul, trying to possess her. Only the priest to whom she'd gone for help, and who'd performed an unsuccessful exorcism, knew what a valiant but losing battle she'd been fighting with the Evil One himself. In yesterday's episode, she finally collapsed and died. Or so everyone believed. John pulled out the drawer in which the body lay, and looked down at his beautiful wife. A tear fell from his eye and landed on Marlena's cheek. Marlena moaned. Her eyes opened. "Marlena!" John cried, throwing his arms around her. "Marlena. Oh my God. Marlena, you're alive!" At the commercial break, my mother explained that what had saved Marlena, what had finally cast the Devil from her, wasn't John's love, really, but her own will to survive.

"Sentimentality," James Baldwin writes in "Everybody's Protest Novel," his critique of *Uncle Tom's Cabin,* "the ostentatious parading of excessive and spurious emotion, is the mark of dishonesty, the inability to feel; the wet eyes of the sentimentalist betray his aversion to experience, his fear of life, his arid heart; and it is always, therefore, the signal of secret and violent inhumanity, the mask of cruelty." In those first days in the hospice, I thought a lot about this definition of sentimentality. I'd always loved it. For over twenty years, I've used it in almost all my classes. I've quoted it to friends, to students. The essay itself has deeply informed my understanding of racism, viewing as it does sentimentality and prejudice as different facets of the same impulse toward abstraction. What we do in relation to our own experience when we think about it sentimentally is similar to what a bigot does when he views someone of another race or religion through the simplifying lens of prejudice—in either case the irreducibly unique and tangled nature of reality is exchanged for some manageable abstraction that tricks us into thinking that everything is figured out, understood, and therefore no longer needs to be examined, considered, looked at freshly, or attended to. Sentimentality, Baldwin suggests, is bigotry internalized, bigotry directed at our own emotions, and prejudice, in turn, is sentimentality writ large.

Much as I still find these implications wonderfully insightful, as I thought about this definition in the context of my sister's dying I began to realize how this definition itself had become for me an abstraction in its own right, unilaterally imposed upon any expression of "excessive or ostentatious parading of emotion," no matter what the context. Without endorsing sentimentality per se, as I thought about how I and my family were responding to my sister's illness, I began to acquire a more particular understanding of the needs and desires that make us vulnerable to sentimentality's appeal. I began to question the concluding phrases of Baldwin's statement, that sentimentality is "always, therefore, the signal of secret and violent inhumanity," that it is always "the mask of cruelty." Certainly this is true of some forms of sentimentality and prejudice, but not all. People aren't sentimental only or primarily because they're cruel or unfeeling. They're sentimental not because their hearts are arid, but because their hearts are too full; not because they're cruel but because they need stability and order, or the illusion of stability and order in the presence of some overwhelming and disruptive truth. More often than not, sentimentality is less a mask of cruelty than a source of anxious comfort.

Immersed as we all were in the bleak facts of experience, in all that terrible immediacy, we wished for any sort of illusory refuge, or palatable lie, that might blunt what we were helpless not to feel. Life, however, would not abide the neat distinctions we desired or assumed between one emotion and another, between the tragic and the comic, the sublime and the petty. Try as we might to simplify it into this or that, life would not permit us anything but a chaotic and exhausting porousness. The coherence of an "arid heart," much as we may have yearned for it at times, was not available.

*   *   *   *

*E*xactly one week after we moved into the hospice was my sister's forty-ninth birthday. My mother and Paula Sanders, a professor of history at Rice and one of Beth's closest friends, went out that morning to find the cake that Gabbi wanted. They had their work cut out for them, for Gabbi asked for a cake that looked like a cheeseburger. We invited a few of Beth's closest friends to join us in the room at the end of the day for a small party. All that morning and into the early afternoon, while Ma and Paula were out shopping, an incredible number of birthday cards arrived for Beth. By three o'clock, there must have been fifty or more of them. After Paula dropped Ma off back at the hospice, and before any of the guests arrived, we gathered around Beth's bed to read the cards to her. Beth wanted us to read only the personal notes and inscriptions, not the generic Hallmark blather.

For more than an hour or so, David and I took turns reading. In card after card, people who had known Beth from almost every period of her life wrote about how important she had been to them: there was a card from a black colleague from the MSU library who remembered how tirelessly Beth had worked on behalf of blacks and other minorities employed by the university. There was a card from an old political crony who remembered what a fierce and effective organizer Beth had been. There was a card from Walter Adams, who was president of Michigan State University in the late sixties, and though he and Beth eventually became good friends in the years that followed, he remembered the 1968 SDS-led occupation of the Army ROTC building, during which, he claimed, Beth kneed him in the groin. "It still hurts, Beth," he wrote, "eighteen years later, and my groin still hurts." "Not true," Beth said, laughing. "I never laid a hand on him. It never happened." There was a card from an old boyfriend who remembered more than anything one evening in particular, just after he had signed the lease on a new apartment but before he'd moved in anything more than a record player and a new LP by Smokey Robinson, how he and Beth danced to that record all night through that empty flat. There was a card from a friend who'd been raped in the early seventies, and she remembered how Beth had taken her in when she "was such a mess," and helped her get back on her feet.

It was hard to read these letters and not break down. I'd get through half of one and then hand it over to David so he could read until he too was overcome. With her eyes closed, Beth listened to us read, and asked us when we'd finished one to read another. My mother listened, though without emotion, stone-faced, as we read these personal and very moving testimonies. Finally Beth had had enough, and said she wanted to sleep.

"Wait," Ma said, handing me an envelope. "Here's a card from Paula. You have to read it."

"But there's no note or inscription, Ma," I said. "Beth only wants to hear the notes."

"But it's from Paula," she said. "She went to a lot of trouble to get that card this morning, and we had so much to do, I'm sure Beth wants to hear it, don't you Beth?"

Beth didn't respond. When it was clear to Ma that I wasn't going to read it, she took the card and read it herself. It was the usual Hallmark fare, fraught with formulaic phrases, generic praise for "your" grace and kindness and other "special qualities" too numerous to mention. Halfway through it, Ma said to Beth, "It's so beautiful. It expresses just how Paula feels about you." "Come on, Ma," I said, "that's not Paula, it's some hack at Hallmark." "It's how she feels," Ma replied, her voice trembling. "It comes from the heart." Then she burst into tears, so overcome she had to leave the room. It was the first time since she'd arrived that I'd seen her break down. Impassively, she had listened to me and David read those poignant letters, those particular stories and individual expressions of appreciation that singly and collectively painted such a concrete and specific picture of who my sister was. But only the idealized abstraction, the sentimental outline, the fill-in-the-blank portrait that could have been anyone under any circumstances, seemed to move my mother. It was the strangest thing I'd ever seen.

And yet not so strange. For my mother, the sending and receiving of cards on birthdays, anniversaries, and other special occasions has always been not just an important social gesture, but the supreme marker of consideration and affection. Over the years, she was never as hurt or angry with her children as on the few occasions when one of us would forget to send her a card on her birthday or Mother's Day. In her moral universe, that was among the most unforgivable of sins. Whenever I'd ask her why she needed something written by an underpaid stranger to believe her children cared about her she would only say, "Because it shows I'm in your thoughts."

But it isn't just the gesture of pulling a card off the shelf at Hallmark and dropping it in the mail that matters to my mother. Rather, or so I've come to think, it is the card itself or the sentimentality it expresses that she needs. The predictable encomiums, the flowery verses, the clichés bespeaking flawless love, all mirror her desire that her life be perfect. And by mirroring that desire, the greeting card perhaps convinces her in some way that it is. So long as she receives a card from us at the appropriate times, she can go on believing that our love for her is as it ought to be, no matter how much we otherwise might disappoint her. In a way, my mother's view of sending and receiving cards is just another expression of her desperate optimism, her refusal to abandon her belief in happiness. She needs cards in the same way that she needs to blame someone for each and every disappointment and disaster—so that, despite what happens, she can think that life is good, perfection possible.

The notes and letters that came with the cards Beth's friends and colleagues sent were tainted with the real. They spoke too directly, in too much specific detail, of personal and social troubles. They presupposed a world in which bad things happen for no good reason, things like rape, like war, like cancer. And while they also spoke of love, courage, loyalty, and grace, those abstractions were embedded (too securely for my mother) in the very sorrows for which they offered compensation.

Later, when I mentioned the incident to Paula, she shook her head, saying she didn't give the card much thought but almost arbitrarily pulled it off the shelf. She said she wanted to write something personal inside it but because the two of them were in a hurry, she simply signed it and gave it to my mother when she dropped her off. My mother assumed that Paula chose the card because it said exactly what she felt about her dying friend. Paula spent almost as much time at the hospice as we did. She spelled me in the evenings when I'd drive my parents back to their hotel. She devoted hours of almost every day running errands for us, or just sitting with us talking. She's a practicing Jew, a wonderful schmoozer, and unlike most Jews of our generation a fluent Yiddish speaker. In these respects, she's very much like my mother, someone with whom my mother could very easily identify. Yet she's like Beth too, being a university professor, an intellectual, a political activist. I wonder when my mother saw her buy that card and simply sign it, and then later when my mother herself read the card to Beth, if Paula didn't become in effect my mother's emissary, a younger version of herself, herself as friend as well as mother to her daughter, ventriloquizing through a stranger's formulaic phrases that a friend had purchased the emotions she could never in her own voice say.

The incident, in Baldwin's terms, was sentimental. But the specific nature of the sentimentalities involved, and the larger context that produced it, were profoundly moving. There was no mask of cruelty here, or violent inhumanity. Fear of life? Yes, but for good reason. An arid heart? No, not for a moment.

*   *   *   *

*T*wo of Beth's colleagues from the library arrived a little before five, carrying a huge poster, which they hung on the wall facing Beth. The poster was bright yellow, splattered everywhere with tiny happy faces. A gigantic birthday card. Everyone on Beth's staff had signed it, some wishing Beth a happy birthday, some telling her how much they loved her, some offering biblical quotations. Someone else from the library showed up with two clown-face balloons, which he attached to the foot of Beth's bed. For Gabbi's benefit, my mother bought cone-shaped party hats, along with the cheeseburger birthday cake. She put a hat on Beth, and gave one to each person as he or she entered the room. More people came than we anticipated. By 5:15, the room was packed. Beth, who had been silent up to then, said, "Here's my sweetie pie" when Gabbi arrived and came up to the bed to kiss her.

There were too many people, and there was too much artificial cheer. Everyone crowded around the bed, chatting to each other, occasionally looking down at Beth, saying a word or two to her in the strained tone of feigned normalcy. Beth looked forlorn and ludicrous in her party hat. I wondered if she even knew she had it on. My mother brought the cake out, which did indeed look like an enormous cheeseburger, a cheeseburger painted by Salvador Dalí, not very appetizing, yet in its weird inappropriateness completely right for the occasion. After we sang "Happy Birthday," and Gabbi blew out the candles for her mother, my mother cut the cake. Gabbi wolfed down two pieces, and then disappeared, as she always did when she visited, into the garden or the family room down the hall. Happy as Beth was to see Gabbi, she didn't seem to notice Gabbi's absence.

My mother was feeding Beth now. Standing on one side of the bed while Paula stood on the other, she was telling Paula how wonderful she thought the supermarkets in Houston were. "Such vegetables," she was saying, "they're not to be believed, and so reasonable." Beth interrupted. She said she wasn't feeling well. My mother could see what was about to happen. She put the plate down, and as Beth vomited she held her two hands out to catch what Beth threw up. "That's all right, honey," she said. "You'll feel better now. Let's get you cleaned up." Paula got a bowl to hold before Beth in case she got sick again while my mother cleaned herself off, then wiped Beth's face. As she did so, she said, "This is too much for Beth. I think everyone should leave."

In a flash, everyone, as they left the room, dumped their plates and party hats in the trash. And the party, mercifully, was over. Almost as soon as the room cleared out, Beth said that the poster was too colorful, it hurt her eyes. So we took it down, and all that remained of the party were the two clowns tethered to the bed, swaying from side to side as my mother continued cleaning up her daughter.

*   *   *   *

Beth woke me in the middle of the night. "Al," she called out, "Al, can you come over here."

"What is it, Beth?" I asked. "Are you uncomfortable? Do you need a boost?"

"No," she said. "It's the ghosts. Make them go away."

"What ghosts, Beth?" Now I was standing by the bed.

"The scary ghosts right there." She was pointing at the clowns. "Make them go away."

I untied the balloons, popped them, and threw away the last remnants of the celebration.

"So, Beth," I said as I lay back down. "How does it feel to be forty-nine?"

And Beth replied, "The only question is, will I live to be fifty?"

*T*wo weeks into the vigil, I made a short trip home to Chapel Hill. My wife had sprained her ankle a few days after I arrived in Houston. It had been three weeks since I had seen my children or my wife, by far the longest time I'd ever been away from home. I was desperate to see them. I felt I had to see them.

Now that David had left for New York, the nights alone with Beth and the days of sitting by her bedside, each day longer than the one before, became unbearably oppressive. More than fifteen people had died in the rooms on either side of and across from Beth's. One day there'd be people going in and out of this or that room, and the next we'd find the door wide open, all the belongings removed, the room completely empty. The only trace that someone had died there, that a family had grieved there, would be a rose the hospice personnel would place as a memorial on the freshly made bed. The rose would lay on the bed for a few hours until another terminal patient was moved in. I was tired of living among the dead and dying. I wanted to be back among the living. I wanted to go home.

On the other hand, I hated leaving my parents, especially now that David too had gone. Of course, all of Beth's friends and colleagues offered to stand in for me, and do whatever my parents needed doing. But I knew my mother and father would be reluctant to ask favors of people they didn't know very well. Even as they encouraged me to go home to my family, I knew they dreaded my absence, even for a day or two. It was impossible not to feel like I was abandoning them. And then, of course, there was Beth. I was fearful that Beth would die while I was gone, that I wouldn't get to say goodbye to her, and that my parents would have to face this last ordeal alone without David or me there to comfort them.

I couldn't get a direct flight on such short notice. On Friday, I'd fly to Raleigh-Durham by way of Detroit, and on Sunday I'd fly to Houston by way of Newark. Both trips would take all day.

I remember almost nothing of the visit except that Nat, who was five at the time, and Isabel, who was three, were very excited to see me, and all that Friday evening and most of Saturday they were simultaneously lovable and impossible to manage. Isabel was too young to comprehend what it really meant that Auntie Beth was very sick and would soon die. She was troubled by my absence, of course, and by my own undisguiseable sadness now that I was home. But unlike Nat she didn't ask me questions about what Beth was going through or what would happen to her when she died. Della told me on the phone the week before that lately Nat had been waking up at night, crying for me. He'd associated or confused Beth's illness with my absence, she said. He'd told her, "I feel like my daddy's dead." He seemed to accept the fact that I had come home for just the weekend, yet over and over he wanted to know when exactly I'd be returning, and though I did my best to reassure him that I'd be home just as soon as I could, his anxiety was no doubt aggravated by my own distracted state of mind. Even while I played with the children, talking with them, looking at the many pictures they had drawn for me while I was gone, my attention would constantly drift back to the hospice, to how Beth was doing, to how my parents were holding up. Even at home, I still felt the need to be in two places at once. By Saturday evening, I was exhausted, happy of course that I was home, but also eager to return to Houston.

That Saturday night, Della and I had tickets to see the Bill T. Jones dance production *Still/Here*. A student of Della's, a dancer herself who was writing her M.A. thesis on a dance production she had choreographed, had gotten us the tickets months ago. Della felt that she at least ought to go, even if I wasn't up to it.

I'd read a little bit about *Still/Here* and Bill T. Jones, and how the dance developed out of the survivor workshops Jones conducted with people around the country dying of AIDS or cancer. I'd heard about the article that Arlene Croce had written in the *New Yorker,* panning the show, even though she hadn't seen it, on the grounds that it was just another manifestation of "victim art," of art that asks us to feel sorry for some oppressed minority, in this case the minority being the terminally ill and those who love them. The emotional coercion of the multimedia production, the dying themselves on video screens telling their harrowing stories while the dancers dance before them, made it impossible for Croce, or anyone, in her view, to respond to the dance as dance, to the art as art.

Della worried that the subject itself would be too painful for me, that it would cut too close to home. But since I couldn't not think about my sister, I thought—why not? Maybe the show would do me good. By reflecting my experience, or something like it, in the medium of dance and story, maybe the show would provide me with a way to understand the formless intensity of what I was feeling then.

In my response to the production, I illustrated everything that Croce feared the show would be. I have no idea if *Still/ Here* was any good artistically. I remember the rapt faces of those who sat around me. I remember how uncomfortable the seat was, how much my back hurt. I remember the dancers themselves less vividly than the taped interviews of the sick, and the images of bodies, especially one seemingly endless wash of breasts on several video screens across the stage. I seem to recall images of scars, too, like the scar on my sister's chest from the mastectomy. In the swirling mix of dance, story, music, and video sounds and sights, I didn't find insight or understanding, only a raw version of my raw emotions. For two hours the stage was one big, busy Rorschach test. From beginning to end, it was all I could do to keep from wailing.

*   *   *   *

As it turned out, the Bill T. Jones Dance Company was on my flight to Newark. At the gate I recognized them instantly, the variety of men and women, white and black, all of different heights and body types, but all sharing the same elegance and grace of movement, even as they stood in line to board. I was standing behind the most remarkable-looking dancer of them all, a tall, very fat, white gay man, whose athleticism and fluidity on stage were all the more apparent for his huge and overweight physique. At one point in the show, he danced all by himself, and while he danced he told the story of his mother's death from cancer. At the curtain call afterward, he received the longest ovation.

While we stood there, waiting to board, I told him that I'd seen the show last night and that I liked it very much. He thanked me. A couple of members of the company turned around to smile. I wanted to say something about my own particular situation, that I was living through the very subject of the show. But before I got a chance to say more, the airline agent announced over the loudspeaker that the flight had been canceled due to some mechanical problem. There were no more flights to Newark that day, so those of us who could should plan to spend the night here in the Raleigh-Durham area and fly out tomorrow. Those of us making connecting flights out of Newark, he said, should get in line at the ticket counter and he would see what he could do.

When the line reassembled at the ticket counter, I was dead last. There were about sixty or seventy people ahead of me. I'm a nervous traveler even at the best of times. But now I was frantic. I had to get back to Houston. There was no way I would not get back today. The line was moving at a glacial pace.

As I started to walk forward, ahead of everybody else, the fat dancer said, "Hey, you're not gonna to cut in line, are you?"

"I have a dying sister!" I blurted out.

"Yeah," he sneered, "Doesn't everybody."

I said "Fuck you," and continued past him, up to the front of the line. Several other members of the company muttered "asshole" and "scumbag." Everyone in the line was furious. I had a letter from the hospice doctor, explaining my sister's situation. I pulled it out and waved it over my shoulder at everyone I passed. The ticket agent took me aside, examined the letter, and immediately got me on a flight to Dallas, with a connecting flight to Houston. I'd get in about an hour later than I was originally scheduled.

The dancers of course had no way of knowing if I told the truth or not. I suppose I'd have responded as they did if someone cut in front of me, especially if I had somewhere important to get to, as they no doubt did. Still, I had to laugh at the vast discrepancy between the well-intentioned work of art designed to raise our sensitivity to the terminally ill and to the loved ones who survive them, and the sneering, skeptical reaction of the dancers to someone who was living the reality of the very dance they did. They've probably performed *Still/Here* a thousand times. I'm certain they all believe profoundly in it as a moral as well as artistic statement. The style of the piece itself, the blending of different media, seems to bespeak a desire to break through the boundary not just between one form of art and another, but also between art and life, the aesthetic and the moral. Yet for the dancers, it seemed that the concern, the sensitivity, the understanding that they danced the night before did not extend beyond the stage itself. The boundary between art and life at that particular moment, to me if not to them, had never seemed so absolute.

I was waiting for the elevator door to open. I had just returned from dropping my parents off at the hotel. It had been an especially hard day. Beth had pretty much stopped taking any nourishment. She was too weak to move her bowels, which were now impacted, and very sore. That afternoon, the nurse had to remove the waste by hand. Beth had been restless, and in pain. In the last few days, whenever I'd ask her if she wanted a boost, she'd tell me no, she didn't. "Why does everybody want to drug me?" Beth was right. We did want to drug her, we wanted her to sleep and not wake up. We wanted her ordeal, and ours, to end. While David and I were sitting in the garden one afternoon, he said he didn't see the point of Beth continuing to live like this. It would be better for all of us if she would just go to sleep. I said that she can still see and touch her daughter. She can kiss Gabbi and be kissed by her. Reduced as her existence was, it was still better than the alternative. But now, two weeks later, even Gabbi had no power to reach her, so far as I could tell. Beth seemed not to respond to any of us. She lay in a coma with her eyes open, flitting from side to side. Who knows what she heard or felt?

That afternoon, my parents and I asked the nurse when she had finished cleaning her how much longer Beth would last. The nurse said Beth could languish for days, even weeks, nobody knows. She said that many of her patients won't die if their families are around. They don't want to die in front of their families, their parents especially, because they know how much their death will hurt them. "Maybe," she advised us, "you should leave Beth for the afternoon. Tell her you're going out to lunch or something, and that you'll be back later in the day. Maybe she needs to be alone to die."

In the abstract, this was probably very good advice. We had no way of knowing what Beth wanted us to do, if our hovering by her bedside, day in, day out, was a comfort to her or another source of pain. When she was still capable of talking and communicating, she never asked us, my parents or me, to go away, whereas she had no compunction telling friends and colleagues that she was tired and wanted them to leave. In health and sickness, she never stood on ceremony with any of us. With her parents especially, she was never shy about telling them about anything they did that bothered or upset her. So I have to assume that our being with her was a comfort. If it weren't, if it were keeping her from finally letting go, we had no way of knowing. All we could do by then was to assume that the person who was dying was the same person we had always known. We had to act toward her in a manner consistent with what we knew about her life and character. Beth had experienced a lot of abandonment throughout her life. She'd been abandoned by her parents, her father in particular, in her late teens and early twenties. She'd been, to some extent, abandoned by her husband in the final stages of her illness. She'd been or felt abandoned by her oncologist. My mother and I were determined that she not feel abandoned by her family in her last days, the nurses' past experience notwithstanding.

Still, it was painful to think that we might be wrong to do this, that the very solace we were offering could be having the opposite effect. It was painful, too, to acknowledge that we wanted her suffering to end, as much for our sake now as hers.

Paula had arrived around eight or so to spell me while I took my parents home. She said that I should take my time. She was happy to stay as long as I needed her to. But my parents that night were tired, and unusually depressed. They didn't want me to come up to the room as I often would, especially when David wasn't here, to relax with them, or eat something. They wanted to sleep. So I dropped them off and headed straight back to the hospice.

Waiting for the elevator, I thought about how much I missed my brother. He'd been back in New York for the past week, and he wouldn't be returning to Houston till Friday. Much as I wanted to spend all my time with Beth, I dreaded being alone with her all through the night. By then, I felt terribly alone and fearful when Beth would wake me, as she often would, moaning, thrashing a little, her head turning from side to side. Sometimes the morphine pump would slip out from beneath the pillow where it was hidden. I'd call the nurse to come and boost her. And while I waited, I would hold the pump and run my finger over the red button that released the morphine. I'd fantasize about pumping all of it into her suffering body, of boosting Beth into another world. Ashamed of what I wanted to do, ashamed as well of being too afraid to do it, I would lie wide awake all night listening to Beth's uneven breathing, counting her every breath, and starting up whenever she would ooh or sigh, unconsciousness as far from me as health was from her body. As I stood waiting for the elevator, I wondered, tired as I was, if I would sleep that night.

Finally the elevator door slid open. I don't know why I always took it. There were only two floors of rooms at the hospice, with a third floor still under construction. And the elevator was incredibly slow. It would have been much quicker to take the stairs. Besides, the elevator's metal walls were painted to look exactly like inlaid blond wood paneling, very Tudor-ish, in keeping with the style of the place, but in the harsh light they shone too garishly, the metallic sheen all the more visible for the costly disguise. Someone, I remember thinking as I pushed the button and began to rise, had spent a lot of money to make the metal cage look very cheap. Anyway, as ugly and slow as the elevator was, I wasn't in a hurry, not that night at least.

When the door slid open I stepped out into a pitch-black empty cavern. The light from the elevator spilled several feet into the vast room and showed a concrete floor, and here and there a ladder, tools, an empty can of Coke next to a stack of insulation, and beyond those few things, and above me, between the ceiling joists, just total darkness that for all I knew could have gone on forever.

I felt like a speck of sentience in outer space, utterly inconsequential, exposed, and isolated. I was staring at my own death, the universe swept clean of me, of my existence. At that moment, the dense web of my loves and commitments was no stronger than the skin of a bubble, through which I could see too clearly the abyss in which it floated.

I stepped back into the elevator. Frantically I kept pressing the "Door Close" button, till the door closed at last, and brought me mercifully back to the second floor. I hurried down the hall to my sister's room. After Paula left, I sat beside Beth, holding her hand for I don't know how long, not so she could feel the warmth of my hand, but so I could feel the warmth of hers.

One night around three o'clock I woke up with a chill. I couldn't find another blanket in the room, so I went out to ask the nurse for one. Opening the door, I was startled to see a crowd of people in the hall, milling in and out of the room across the way. All African Americans, they were dressed up, the men in suits, the women in dresses. They held glasses of what looked like champagne or white wine. Several small kids dressed to the nines were there as well, playing among the grown-ups. Everyone I noticed seemed to be laughing and talking. And there was gospel music coming from the open room. I asked one of the celebrants, an old man who was sitting on a bench outside the room, if it was someone's birthday, and he looked at me a moment, then got up without answering and went into the room.

As I passed by, I saw more people standing around the bed. The woman lying there was utterly still, and ashen. You knucklehead, I said to myself, the woman's dead. That's why they're here. No wonder the old man didn't answer.

In the days or weeks that she'd been here at the hospice, her relatives had kept the door shut on their vigil. This was the first time I'd gotten a glimpse of her. It dawned on me that we too had kept our door closed. So did almost everybody in the hospice. Why? I wondered as I hurried by to get my blanket. Was it only privacy? Or was it also that we didn't want to see how other people died, how other families grieved? Did we want to keep our sorrow hidden from outsiders, so we could think that it was ours alone, utterly unlike anybody else's? Maybe we thought that if we couldn't cling to or preserve the particular, the unique, the never-to-be-repeated person that Beth was, then we could cling at least to what was wholly ours and unlike anybody else's in our grief for her. Unable to resist the inexorability of her dissolution, the impersonality of her disease, the anyone-ness of the flesh as it disintegrates, weren't we resisting as best we could the reduction of our sorrow to a general process no different in our case from the sorrow that the nurses, the doctors, and the social workers had seen day in, day out, year after year, in every other room? In this resistance in the name of difference, weren't we most like everybody else?

Now that the woman had died, her door stood open. And what I saw was completely unexpected. Even the people who were crying in the hall weren't only crying; they were also chatting convivially with one another, and even laughing from time to time. Even those gathered around the woman's bedside displayed a range of feelings that didn't conform to my idea of sorrow. I thought about the woman lying there before her family, now the inert object of their glances, of the words they exchanged, of the stories they were no doubt telling. I remembered that for Jews it is profoundly disrespectful to leave a corpse uncovered. In our tradition, death means the end of reciprocity, which is the soul of life. No one should have to suffer being looked at if he or she cannot return the gaze.

As I thought about these differences, it occurred to me that maybe we, my family at least, were keeping our doors closed not in order to protect our sense of being different, but to keep from seeing how pervasive difference was, that difference was itself the norm, that there was nothing special in it. Maybe that's what troubled us.

The nurse gave me two blankets in case one wasn't enough. As I made my way back through the crowd, the old man stopped me. Smiling, he handed me a plastic glass of wine. He said I looked like I could use one. I put the blankets down on the bench. And as we stood there drinking together, I in my sweatpants and t-shirt, he in his black suit, he told me that his sister, Thomasina, had lived a good life, a Christian life, and they were celebrating her coming home to Jesus. "The Good Lord don't send us nothin' we can't bear," he said. "Oh, she suffered somethin' terrible, terrible, but the end was peaceful, and all her babies, and her babies' babies, they was here with her to see her off."

I told him about Beth, and her cancer, how hard it was for all of us, but especially for Ma and Dad. He nodded. He said that when his own child died now twenty years ago his preacher told him a story about Sarah, how the Lord was angered with her for laughing at Him when He promised her she'd have a child in her old age, and that her punishment would be that she'd outlive that child. He didn't know if it was true or not, he didn't know his scripture like he ought to, but he himself hadn't been living a Christian life in those days, and the story helped him understand what the Lord was doing to him, why He'd take his son like that.

I knew the story, or one like it. It wasn't from the Bible but from somewhere else: was it Louis Ginzburg's *The Legends of the Jews*? or a Talmudic commentary? And did it have to do with Sarah, or some other Jewish matriarch? I couldn't remember, but as the old man reminded me of it, I thought that maybe I would tell it to my parents, not so they'd draw from it the moral that the old man drew—that God was punishing them for their past sins—but rather so they'd know their devastating sense of loss had long been recognized within their cultural traditions. I thought it might solace them to know that a matriarch of their religion had suffered what they were suffering now.

Of course I didn't tell him I was Jewish. And maybe I didn't have to. He probably knew himself that his form of consolation, like his form of grief, could not be mine. But despite our differences, or maybe it was because of them, as we stood there drinking in the middle of the night, among his family, his sister's body still warm in the bed behind us, her soul to him and all his family now translated to a better place, I felt drawn to the old man and found myself wanting to reciprocate his stories with stories of my own. I told him about me and Beth, how close we were, and how much I would miss her. I told him about Russ's history, how his own mother had died when he was five of the same cancer that was killing Beth, and how much trouble he was having dealing with it all. When I mentioned Gabbi, the old man said he'd seen her here from time to time, and that, as hard as things were, he could tell she had a lot of lovin' in her family, and repeated, "The Good Lord don't send us nothin' we can't bear."

I finished my drink, and thanked him. He said he was sorry for my loss, and that he hoped I and my family, and "that little girl" especially, would find the peace he'd found. I picked up the blankets and went on down the hall. Holding the door open with one hand, I looked back at the party. The old man smiled and waved before returning to his sister's room, as I returned to Beth's, the door now slowly closing shut behind me.

Gabbi almost never came to visit Beth without a friend in tow. Arriving in the early evening after horseback-riding camp, she'd kiss her mother, and then she and whichever friend she came with would go out to the garden or the family room to play. She didn't cling to Beth; she didn't show much feeling of any kind around her. And while she never stayed in the room for very long, she never balked at coming, so long as she could bring somebody with her. Gabbi is a spirited child, energetic, restless, her need for physical activity nearly inexhaustible. Even after her long days at the stables in the awful heat and humidity of a Houston summer, she showed no signs of slowing down. We, of course, were too tired and distracted to keep her entertained. Besides, what was there to do for any child, much less one so restless, among so many somber people in the room of her dying mother?

But the friend she brought with her did more than merely entertain her. Or so it seemed to me. In bringing her, Gabbi brought her ordinary world into the strange and frightful world of death and dying. Much as she wanted to see her mother at the end of every day, much as she needed proof that she still had a mother, I think her mother symbolized for her, by then, complete disruption, the fragility of every-thing that made her feel at home and safe. As a defense against the terror and confusion she must have felt in the presence of her dying and now mostly unresponsive mother, she needed, it seemed, a continual reminder of the reliable and settled pleasures that made up her life. If the hospice was a place where she could play with friends, just like she did at home, then maybe she could feel more certain that the world, as she had known it, would survive her mother's death.

Most mornings I'd go over to the house. As soon as I arrived, Russ would leave for the Wellness Center, where, to strengthen his ailing heart, he worked out under the supervision of a physical therapist. Before Beth's condition worsened, he'd been working out two or three times a week, but now he was going every day. In the face of so much of what he couldn't control, of so much overwhelming pain and sadness, he retreated to the gym and concentrated his attention on his body, on keeping himself as well as he could, for his own sake and for Gabbi's.

For an hour or so until I'd drive her to the stables, Gabbi would entertain me. With broomsticks, mops, and dowels laid across cushions, she set up hurdles for a jumping course in the open area between the living room and dining room. She'd turn on her favorite country and western station and, pretending to be a horse, she'd gallop through the course, jumping every hurdle, singing as she went. She was incredibly graceful as she ran the course. Some of the hurdles were two or three feet high but she had no trouble clearing them. As a horse, she seemed relaxed and confident; in motion, as she always was, but now so calm, even serene, she had none of the jumpy restlessness and hyperkinetic unpredictability that made her sometimes very tiring to be around. Her body seemed at one with her activity, not straining anxiously against it, possessing the same focus and concentration it possessed when she was either riding or caring for the horses at the stables.

I loved watching her jump from hurdle to hurdle, always in rhythm to the song that she was singing. Many of the songs she sang were quintessential country and western, fraught with heartache, hard luck, and betrayal, but as she sang them, jumping from hurdle to hurdle, she seemed to take all that twangy sorrow into her body and convert it into elegance and mastery.

Later, I would linger at the stables, watching her as she moved among the horses. They all seemed so huge next to Gabbi. Yet as she brushed them down, or rode them English or western style, it amazed me how responsive they were to her, and she to them, how intimately she seemed able to converse with all their massive strength and power. The pleasure was part and parcel of the discipline.

Watching her ride, I'd think what a strange time for Gabbi this must be. Like Beth, and like my mother, she too must have felt abandoned by her parents. Her mother was gone, for all intents and purposes, and her father was withdrawn, preoccupied, distracted. He spent his mornings working out, caring for his damaged heart, and in the evenings he'd arrange for Gabbi to spend the night at someone's house or for someone to spend the night at hers. In either case, he made sure she was constantly occupied, involved with someone other than himself. Happy as she was to ride each day, or always to have a friend around her, there still seemed something desperate in her happiness, as if she sought in her specific pleasures not just a compensating refuge from a double feeling of abandonment, but a compensating discipline, a compensating structure. Riding her horses, or grooming them, did she get to be a kind of parent? Or pretending to be a horse when she would play alone or with her friends, did she imagine she was parenting herself?

During those four weeks Gabbi got to do whatever she wanted, and in an odd way she did seem extremely happy, yet I wonder if the happiness itself didn't trouble her, since it came at a time when everybody else around her had never seemed so sad. I wonder if the very things that made her happy didn't also make whatever fear and sorrow she herself felt for her mother all the more confusing. In her seven-year-old mind, what bizarre ambivalent connection did she draw among getting to do the things she most wanted to do whenever she wanted to do them, her mother's death, and her own feeling of abandonment? However much the pleasure she pursued with such intensity provided her with refuge from what she couldn't understand, however much it helped her find some compensating sense of order and stability for the disorder all around her, did pleasure also in its own right become a source of pain? Did it become at one and the same time the shelter she was seeking, and another aspect of the storm that she found shelter from?

In any event, as confusing as this period surely was for Gabbi, once her mother had finally passed away, and the "party" ended, and she wasn't spending every waking minute at the stables, or having friends around her all the time, and all of us returned to our own families—once she and Russ had crossed the threshold to their new existence and had to settle into what their lives would be, alone, without Beth, without the rest of us around, from day to ordinary day, only then, it seemed to me, would she have to come to terms as best she could with the complicated legacy of what she'd gone through. Only later, when life was "normal" once again, would her troubles really start.

Several hours before Beth died, early in the afternoon, Russ came by the hospice to okay Beth's obituary. One of her colleagues in the sociology department had written a draft of it and sent it on to us for our approval.

Russ stood by Beth's bedside a moment, listening to her erratic breathing. Then he said, "That's Cheyne-Stokes breathing."

"What?" I asked.

"Cheyne-Stokes," he said. "I remember the name from my days as a paramedic. That's what it's called, Cheyne-Stokes breathing. Gonna be anytime now. Anytime."

Anytime, though, so the nurse on duty told us, could mean today, tomorrow, this week, or next week. But Russ was certain death was nearer. And that day, for the first time since Beth was moved here, he didn't leave. For the remainder of the afternoon, until after six, he sat beside Beth, either holding her hand, or just watching her, or staring out the window. A half hour or so before he left, he said he wanted to be alone with Beth. That evening he didn't bring Gabbi by. I realized after he was gone that he never got around to looking at the obituary.

David, who'd returned from New York a few days earlier, took Ma and Dad back to the hotel around seven o'clock. Each night for four weeks now, they'd said farewell to Beth as if for the last time. The solemnity of these fare-wells, however, didn't preclude moments of high, if inad-vertent, comedy. The night before, for instance, after my mother kissed Beth and told her she would see her "bright and early in the morning," my father went over to the bed. Because he's virtually blind in one eye, he wears an audio watch, a watch that announces the hour in a digitized voice that's part telephone operator, part Minnie Mouse. Never having learned how to reset it, he leaves the watch on Cali-fornia time. So the irritation of hearing Minnie Mouse an-nounce the time every hour on the hour was doubled by the fact that she was always giving us the wrong time. Dad could never say goodbye to Beth without crying. And none of us could watch him lean over to kiss her without choking up ourselves. But this night, just as his lips touched hers, Minnie proclaimed, "It is now five o'clock. The time is five o'clock." To make matters worse, his hand accidentally rested on the bed's control panel, and as he kissed her, the bed kicked into gear, and Beth's legs started to rise. "Dad," I said, running up to him, "Dad, let go." And he looked up, confused, his hand still on the button. "What's the mat-ter?" he asked. "What the hell is wrong?" Beth looked like a partially closed jackknife, her legs now higher than her head. I gently took his hand off the control panel, and low-ered the bed to its original position. David and Ma were laughing. My father too by now was laughing, crying and laughing at the same time. Even though Beth was uncon-scious, once everyone had left I whispered in her ear, "If you weren't dying, Beth, you'd have loved this."

By nine o'clock, her breathing seemed particularly la-bored. The tip of her tongue was visible in the corner of her mouth, which was otherwise closed, sucking what air it could into her body while her chest shuddered as it rose and fell. The nurse assured David and me that, despite whatever was happening in and to her body, Beth could not feel anything, not with the amount of morphine in her system. In effect, her mind, such as it was, was wholly cut off from the rest of her.

The next few hours passed as a single moment. David and I stood on either side of the bed. For much of the time, David held one hand, I held the other. From time to time, David would say he loved her, she should let go, it's okay now, you can just let go. I couldn't speak. All I could do was look on in amazement at the mystery as it unfolded, or enfolded. I squeezed Beth's hand, feeling its still vital but beleaguered warmth; I watched her half-open eyes flitting from side to side. Already lusterless, they seemed to sink back into their sockets. Her face seemed smaller too, less bloated suddenly, at once more like the face I'd always known and stranger, hardly hers at all, as the life within her petered out. I thought about the cells within her body, the good cells, struggling to stay alive, and the bad ones still proliferating, now on the verge of their total but absurd victory. I thought about Sherwin Nuland's metaphor for cancer as a sort of adolescent hooliganism, the cells hypersexed like teenagers, asocial, irresponsible, raiding the body's lifeblood so they can go on reproducing, reproducing so they can reproduce. And where in all that biological "wilding" was my sister's soul? Was it still clinging to "the dying animal," its only home, or had it already disengaged, moved on, to where, or what?

I thought about reincarnation. Even if it were true, what comfort could there be in thinking that my sister might return as a firefly, or a deer foraging in the woods behind my house, or even as another person. Even imagining a heaven, or an afterlife of some kind or other, in which we all get reabsorbed into undifferentiated spirit, even that would mean the end of who we are in time and space, the end of all we've been to one another. What good could Heaven do me now? Could it make the loss of this particular flesh less absolute? It's not the soul, it's no eternal essence, abstract and removable, but the vitally opaque, contingent, and never-to-be-repeated flesh we love and cling to, the flesh we mourn. To imagine my sister's soul as existing separately from her body is to imagine no one and nothing I have ever known or ever could know. For me, there is as little consolation in the thought of that as in the thought of death as pure extinction.

Now and again Beth would try to cough, but the muscles in her throat were too weak, and the cough would seem to lodge there in her vocal chords and go no further. Yet in that phlegmy wheezing, I could hear her voice, or the faintest echo of it, barely discernible but still discernible as hers and no one else's, but now coming from some inconceivably distant place within her. At that moment, her voice became a figure for the soul, for a soul I could imagine and believe in as a bodiless exhalation bearing the body's unmistakable but evanescent trace.

*   *   *   *

By midnight, Beth seemed to breathe more easily, or seemed to need less breath. Her tongue was still protruding from the corner of her mouth, but her chest rose and fell less violently, like an athlete's after some great exertion at the moment when his breathing starts to slow. Ever concerned with the theatrics of an occasion, David dimmed the lights. Each breath came more weakly now than the one before. Then Beth breathed in, and didn't breathe out. We thought this was it, that she was gone, but thirty or forty seconds later, she exhaled and as she did she let out one long, deep, and profoundly eerie moan. It was an unearthly sound, for there was no voice to it at all, nothing in it I could recognize as Beth, but something anterior to personality, to human life itself. Oddly enough, what I thought of when I heard it was the Iliad, and how, according to Homer, whenever someone dies in battle the soul leaves the body through the mouth. Surely it's this sound that Homer had in mind. To both David and me, it was the sound of the spirit moving on. The sound was beautiful to David, beautiful and consoling, whereas to me, always too ready to mourn, the sound personified reluctance, sorrow, anguish, the flesh in its final sentience crying out, Not this, please, anything but this.

That moan, I'm certain, marked the end of Beth, the end of life, though the body went on breathing for another minute or so, each breath a little fainter, weaker, the body's electricity guttering down, dissolving, till there was no breath at all. What remained on the bed was already turning ashen. Right up to that last moan, she was still my sister. But this was nobody I knew. The suddenness and absoluteness of the change had caught me unawares. Much as I knew her death was coming, much as I had waited for this moment, and imagined it, now that it was here it was the last thing I expected in the world, the last thing I was ready for.

David didn't want anyone to see Beth with her head slumped to one side, her jaw slack, her eyes open. For the last few days, he had stayed close to her bedside, holding her hand, stroking her arm, touching her without squeamishness or hesitation. As I watched him, it occurred to me that what appeared before as inhibition may also have been a sign of respect. Given his history with Beth, it could be that he assumed she didn't want such intimacy from him. He may have held back for fear that she'd refuse him. Once she couldn't refuse, his inhibition vanished. As he had for the last few days, he touched her now with a sense of privilege and gratitude. He gently closed her eyes. He straightened her head on the pillow. He propped another pillow up against her chin to keep her mouth from opening. He administered these intimate last rites to his sister, restoring her with his own hands to an appearance of dignity.

When David had finished, we sat in silence for a long while. Then we informed the nurses, who noted the time of death and called the undertakers. David called Ma and Dad. I called Russ. He was awake. He'd been waiting for the call. He didn't ask for details. He didn't need them. He said he'd bring Gabbi by the hotel in the morning so that all of us could be together. His voice sounded full of sorrow and completely numb. Though he had spent less time at the hospice than the rest of us, he knew before any of us did when Beth would die. Back in May, Beth predicted Russ would withdraw as her illness worsened. She said he had his own way of dealing with things, his own way of showing love and grief, and she asked us, my mother and me, to respect that. He had been through so much in the last two years. He had his own heart disease to deal with, and his wife's long illness, during most of which, alone, without anybody's help, he nursed her patiently, devotedly. Throughout that period, too, as throughout his life, he had to live with all that racial pain. In those last weeks, once my mother and I had arrived, he'd earned the right, if anybody had, to withdraw into himself, to ready himself in his own way for life as a single parent, as a widower. I know Beth understood this. I'd like to think that she died knowing that he'd been there with her throughout that final afternoon. I wanted to tell him this, and so much else, but all I could say was I was sorry for his pain, and he said, "Yeah, I know."

The nurse told us we could leave Beth's things in the room tonight but we would need to have the room cleared out by early morning. David said he didn't want to come back to the hospice, he wanted to clean the room out now. He also wanted to get away before the undertakers arrived. He went into frantic overdrive. He got a couple of plastic bags from the nurses' station and dumped everything into them, Beth's two or three nightgowns, her toothbrush, her reading glasses, all of the cards and letters, magazines, a picture of Gabbi. He remembered that he'd put a load of laundry in the dryer earlier that night, and he ran down the hall to check it. He came back a moment later, his arms full of damp clothes. "Fuck it," he sighed, "it would take too long to run another cycle." So he slipped on a damp t-shirt and damp jeans, and while I stood by Beth's bed one last time, he carried everything out to the car.

"Come on, Al," he said, "we gotta get out of here," his hand now on my shoulder. I kissed Beth's already-cooling forehead. Looking at her one last time, I said to myself, someone, probably tonight, will clean the room, and by early morning there'll be a rose here on the pillow where Beth's head has lain. By the afternoon, another man or woman will occupy the bed. Another family will wait as we waited. By tomorrow, there'll be no trace of Beth, of what she suffered, or of any of our sorrow as we watched her all through those days and weeks that seemed as if they'd never end, and soon would seem as if they'd never happened.

* * * *

Was Beth's a "good" death? To answer yes too confidently would be to ignore the pain and physical indignities she suffered. "Easy for you to say," I hear her tell me. And yet to answer no would be to overlook so much of what happened in those last four weeks. The sociology award, the extraordinary number of letters she received on her birthday testifying to her importance in so many people's lives, the endless stream of visitors, of calls—all of these honors and expressions of love convinced Beth that she had lived if not a happy life (whatever that is), then a life that mattered. But there was more than this. There were the changes that occurred within Beth and between Beth and the family, my parents especially, that were supremely valuable. She had the gift of all my mother's inexhaustible ministrations, and she gave my mother, in return, the gift of knowing that she'd been the best of mothers to her daughter, a gift I think my mother wanted more than anything in the world.

Beth also had the gift of reconciliation with her father. Over the years, there'd been so much trouble between them. Not just the disownment and the years of silence afterward, but even earlier, and later, his relentless disapproval and rigidity, and refusal to accept anything about her life except those things (i.e., her professional accomplishments) that made him look good in the eyes of his own friends and family. "He loves my résumé," Beth used to say, "not me." And yet they got beyond that history in the end. In May when Beth was first told she was terminally ill, and we'd come out to be with her, we were sitting in the living room one evening after dinner. We were talking about our plans for the next few months, how Beth would spend her final summer. At one point she said she hoped we'd use her illness as an opportunity to treat each other better, to take better advantage of the time we have. "Maybe," she said, laughing ruefully, "my death will satisfy the family's quota of bad luck, so that none of the rest of you will have to go through anything as bad as this. Think of me as your sacrificial lamb." My father broke down. He asked her for the first time if she could ever find it in her heart to forgive him for his stupidity and prejudice, "for all the years I threw away." He'd given her his remorse, and she'd answered it, as she went over and embraced him, with her forgiveness.

Apart from this and other reconciliations and acceptances, with Ma, with David, with me as I learned from her to overcome my own aversion to her suffering and show my love for her through touch, through doing nothing but simply listening, simply being with her as I massaged her head, her neck and shoulders, or held her hand for hours at a time, Beth's death or dying was good in another way as well. She had a pleasure all of us, I think, as children dream of having. She, in effect, attended her own funeral before she died and got to hear her eulogy.

In May she said she wanted me to do the eulogy at her memorial service. I worked on it throughout the first three weeks of the hospice vigil. I finished it the day before Beth slipped into a coma. The hospice doctor told us that maybe Beth was holding on because of some unfinished piece of business, it could be something metaphysical, some problem she's working out inside her, or, he said, it could be something simple, like some assurance that a bill's been paid, or the funeral arrangements have all been made. Given that Beth told the rabbi that she could die in peace if she were certain that her house was all in order, and how anxious she'd been about getting the memorial service planned out in advance, I thought that it might comfort her to know that we had gotten everything arranged just as she wanted, right down to the eulogy itself, which, she told me, she wanted to be funny as well as intimate.

It was the middle of the afternoon. For some reason, I was alone with Beth, an unusual occurrence during the daytime. I told her I had written her eulogy, and did she want to hear it. She nodded. So I nervously began to read. I wrote about her sense of humor and how, until her final illness, her wit had almost never expressed itself directly in jokes that she herself would tell so much as in her willingness to laugh when someone else was being funny. That Beth was much more comfortable in the audience laughing at a joke than in the spotlight telling one, I went on to say, was partly an expression of her generosity of spirit, and partly an expression of a lack of confidence, a specific symptom of a more general and wholly unjustified insecurity about how interesting she believed herself to be. Despite her professional abilities and accomplishments, I wrote, when it came to personal relationships, Beth "wrongly assumed that in a room full of people she'd almost always be the least deserving of attention." Yet all this seemed to change in the last weeks of her life. "Virtually paralyzed with cancer, flat on her back Beth became a stand-up comic." I told the story of her run-in with the evangelical woman in St. Luke's Hospital, how Beth had countered that woman's condescending piety with Janis Joplin's "prayer." I also told another story, how one night when Paula visited, they heard a patient in another room begin to howl and moan. Beth said, "You hear that man across the hall? That man has followed me from Methodist, to St. Luke's, to here. I can't believe I'm being stalked by a terminally ill man." (Thereafter, Beth referred to him as the Terminal Stalker.)

I glanced at Beth from time to time, but her eyes were closed, and her face showed no expression. What did she feel as she listened to me describe her in the past tense? Did my portrait contradict her sense of who she was, or reinforce it? Did it console or frighten? My voice trembling with a weird mix of sorrow, honor, and uncertainty, I read the final sentences about how Beth was more than just a comic in her last days, and more than just a teacher who showed us how to face up to the worst life has to offer, for the teacher in those last days learned a few things too. Because of how her friends and colleagues rallied around her, because of all the devotion everyone had shown her, Beth was astonished and deeply moved to learn at last that she was someone worthy to be loved, that she deserved to be admired, honored, and, finally, cared for so completely. Here's how I concluded: "There's a tradition in Orthodox Judaism that says that when we die, the soul goes up to Heaven to study Torah for eternity with God. Well, if there's Torah study in Heaven, there must be books, and if there are books in Heaven, there must be a library, and if there's a library, someone must direct it. And who better qualified for that top position than my sister Beth."

I don't know how much of this Beth heard or understood. But when I finished reading, she seemed to smile. She lifted one hand slightly off the bed, and put her forefinger and her thumb together, as if to say "Yes, that'll do just fine."

*A*fter the memorial service, I picked up Beth's ashes from the funeral home. On the way back to the house where friends and family were already gathering, with the urn beside me on the passenger seat, I switched on the radio, which was tuned to a black station that played nothing but soul and Motown. I recognized the song from the opening chords—"Ain't No Mountain High Enough," by Marvin Gaye and Tammy Terrell. "Hey, Beth, one of your favorites," I said to the urn beside me, and as I sang along, I thought of Beth and Russ's wedding back in 1988, and how we all danced in a soul train to that song and countless other Motown hits throughout the night.

Beth was six months pregnant with Gabbi at the time. She and Russ had tried for more than two years to get pregnant. They consulted fertility specialists, they tried different forms of artificial insemination, and eventually, assuming that she'd waited too long (Beth at the time was in her early forties), they gave up. As so often happens, almost as soon as they had, Beth got pregnant. And they decided to get married before the baby came.

Della and I were the only members of our family who attended. My father refused to go to Michigan either for the wedding or for the birth. My mother, out of respect for him, stayed home. She planned to come out later in the fall after the baby was born. David was "between jobs" at the time and couldn't afford to come.

They were married in their own home in Lansing. Only family attended the ceremony itself. But that night they threw a huge bash. Over a hundred people came to the house, almost all of Russ's family, and many of his old friends from college and high school. Many of Beth's college friends were there (all of them veterans of the antiwar movement). Almost all of her colleagues from the MSU library, where she was deputy director, came, and others whom she'd befriended in her more than twenty years at MSU, many of the same people who would write to her so movingly on her last birthday—people like Walter Adams, or the woman who'd been raped, and even the old boyfriend who described how the two of them had danced one evening through his empty flat.

And yet as festive as the party was, the real celebration didn't take place until later in the night, when the dancing started. The music was strictly Motown—the Four Tops, the Temptations, Smokey Robinson and the Miracles, Martha Reeves and the Vandellas, Gladys Knight and the Pips, Marvin Gaye—the very songs I used to listen to behind my father's back throughout the sixties, the songs to which my sister introduced me, and by which during her years of banishment I affirmed (if only to myself) my loyalty to her.

Beth and Russ were the first to dance. What was the song? "Can't Help Myself"? "Too Busy Thinkin' 'bout My Baby"? "The Watusi"? "Heat Wave"? "Dancin' in the Streets"? I can't recall but as I drove back with her ashes from the funeral home, I told myself that it was this song, these words: "There ain't no mountain high enough, ain't no valley low enough, ain't no river wide enough, to keep me from gettin' to you, girl. . . ." I could see Beth, six months pregnant in her white dress, dancing in that understated way of hers, quietly graceful, without flamboyance, as if reluctant, even then, to call too much attention to herself, but now she has one arm akimbo, the other raised, one finger pointing, wagging at her husband as she mouths the words, "If you're ever in trouble, I'll be there on the double . . . ," and the rest of us move out onto the dance floor, forming ourselves into a soul train behind the two of them, dancing wherever they dance, around the dining-room table, through the living room, upstairs now, now down, all of us, white and black, singing together, dancing, each in our own way, to the same song, in celebration of my sister and her husband, of their union, and of all the blessings still to come.

Afterwords:
Poems

SCREE

Long scree of pill bottles
    spilling over the tipped brim
of the wicker basket, fifty or more,
    a hundred,

your name on every one and under
    your name the brusque rune of instructions—
which ones to take, how many, how often,
    on what days,

with or without food, before or
    after eating, impossible
toward the end to keep them all straight,
    not even

with your charts, your calendars, the bottles
    ranged in sequence along the kitchen
counter—you always so
    efficient,

organized, never without a plan,
    even when planning had come down
to this and nothing more, for there was
    still a future

in it, though the future reached
    only from one bottle to
the next, from pill to pill, each one
    another

toe-hold giving way
        beneath you on the steep slope
you never stopped struggling against,
        unable not

to climb, and then, when climbing
        was impossible, not to try slowing
the quickening descent. You had
        descended now,

your body thinned to the machine
        of holding on, while I exhausted
by the vigil, with all your medicine
        spread before me,

looked for something, anything
        at all to help me sleep. To help me
for a short while anyway
        not be

aware of you, your gaunt hand
        clutching the guardrail, your eyes
blind, flitting, scanning, it seemed,
        the air above them

for their own sight, and the whimper
        far back in the throat, the barely
audible continuous
        half cry half

wheeze I couldn't hear and not think
        you were saying something, though
I couldn't make out what. I wanted
        to sleep,

I wanted if just for that one night
	to meet you there on that steep slope,
the two of us together, facing
	opposite

directions, I, because I wasn't
	dying, looking down, desiring
what you, still looking up, resisted,
	because you were.

HAND

You all but paralyzed, leashed to the catheter
that almost decorously slipped out from beneath the
    blanket,
running down under the guardrails to the urine bag

that no longer filled, since you'd stopped eating, drinking,
the body nearly now past feeding on itself,
past even that much agency—yet days before,

you were still able to get yourself up out of bed.
Dizzy with morphine that by then could only dull
the pain, not kill it, with your arm around my shoulder,

no matter how it hurt, you were determined to walk,
because you still could, to the bathroom, to complete
the marathon of five feet maybe, maybe six,

and on your own relieve yourself, and clean yourself,
and on your own stand up, and hug the nightgown to you
so it wouldn't slip from your shoulders, your privacy
    preserved,

protected, clung to, till you were safely back in bed.
Each stage of your decline, if it was hell
while you were in it, did it become too brief a heaven

once it had passed, as walking first, then privacy,
had passed, as these, too, would pass, these final vestiges
of will, of purpose, relief, if not exactly pleasure,

in the hand you, all but paralyzed, could barely lift,
but lifted, trembling, only inches from the bed
where it could flex, unflex, the fingers slowly closing

halfway toward the bony hollow of the palm,
closing and opening each time a little farther,
easier, until the numbness in the joints began

to loosen and retreat, and the hand could feel again
still capable of soothing itself, of being soothed,
before it fell at last like dead weight back to the bed?

ROSE

The pump lay under the pillow where no one could see it.
Those nights when the morphine it released was not
        enough
to let her sleep, and Beth moaned weakly, thrashing a
        little,
turning her head from side to side, the pump would slip
out from beneath the pillow, dangling from her shoulder
where the thread-thin tube went in. Before I'd call the
        nurse,
I'd hold it in my hand. Its case, the size and shape
of the TV's remote control. I'd run my finger down
across the flat red button, trembling just to graze it,
cool as metal to the touch, yet so secure,
so tight within its socket that I could press on it lightly,
and then less lightly, and still it wouldn't budge. Ooh,
Beth would mutter over and over through pursed lips,
ooh, her tremulous weak syllable of no ease,
ooh, and please, and if I pumped all of it out
into the suffering engine of her, so she at last
could sleep, so I too could sleep, who'd know? Who'd
        blame me?
Rose-red, the button was, flat bloom of coolest fire,
in the half dark. When the nurse arrived to "boost" her,
that's what she called it, I'd leave the room, I'd walk the
        halls
to calm myself, to quell the shame of what I wanted
to do, the shame of being too afraid to do it—and here
and there I'd pass a room someone had died in

earlier that day. The door that had been kept shut
up to then, as ours was shut (was it to guard
our sorrow, by hiding it to think it ours alone,
peculiar to ourselves?), the door stood open now
because it opened onto no one, nothing, gone
the bouquets on the shelves, the pitiful toiletries,
cards on the feeding tray, pictures of children, all
the unbearable weight of each particular dying gone,
effaced, a gauze of sorrow swept thoroughly away,
and what remained was just the bed's amnesia,
immaculate white counterpane, white sheet, white
    rounded pillow,
and like a still opening red rupture on the void
it seemed to brighten from, absurdly beautiful,
where only hours before the head had lain, a rose.

AIR

The Mexican woman in the room across from Beth's;
the teenage boy down the hall, the young man in the
    corner
room so shrivelled beneath the covers that the bed
looked always just made, smooth as if no one was in it;

the man in the next room who for days had been
    delirious,
violent, and after trying to choke his wife
whom he didn't recognize, had to be strapped down
until the tumor in his brain became restraint enough;

the black man with lung cancer who could have been
my age or my father's, and who, when he still could,
with his walker first, and then with his wheelchair, day
and night patrolled the halls wheezing as he asked each

person, anybody, even the nurses, for a smoke,
a puff, come on, man, who's gonna know the difference;
and Beth herself, of course, all of the dying, each one,
in turn, when the end was near, would look away from us,

their faces drawn toward the window, toward the light
    outside,
more flower now than human, but still human, yearning
not for people, though—they seemed all done with that—
and not for grace, or mercy, or for any otherworldly

health, but only this, the air outside, the opalescent
flux of shade and sun dazzle there on the skin
as the body moves again and breathes in what is
always opening out around it wherever it goes.

THE TABLE

Here is the phantom solace of a table,
shimmer of candlelight in every glass,
at every place an incandescent hovering
out of nowhere of somebody's face,

amnesia of the iron dark receding
bit by bit as feature after feature
shapes all around you brief fluorescences
of recognition, flickering on and off,

and for a moment you are niece again
in those eyes, friend in those, acquaintance, cousin,
granddaughter, great-granddaughter, on and on
the faces dimmer as they stretch away

into irrelevance along the table,
each one your emissary now, the closest,
the most remote, all burnishing the dark
to different shades of this familial dream,

this dream of mine, what I have left to give you:
Now you can sit among them, unafraid,
not minding even as the obsolete
distinctions they've put on to welcome you

begin dissolving, and you lift the glass
they lift, and drink the wine they drink, and see
your lips now anybody's lips reflected
in the wine you lower as they lower it.

THE SUMMONING

There is the room. There is the fire in the grate,
sap fizzling out loose tentacles of steam
along the fluent borders of the burning,

its light diffusing as it grades away
to darkness an unwavering presumption
not of my somehow being here again,

but of my never having left. The way
each thing so certain of itself as mine
as I arranged it still assumes my seeing

with an ordinary absent-mindedness,
the way the carpet's crushed pile signifies
the pressure of my heel, the dented pillow—

the posture and exact weight of a pleasure
that isn't pain subsiding but the body's
still undisproved belief that this is only

another evening after a long day,
a squandering on myself of instances
I have no end of. Even the calm implies

only the minor havoc of what might soon
disperse it: Isn't there dinner to prepare?
Couldn't the phone ring at any moment?

Where is my daughter? What is it I've forgotten?
Whose version of myself is this? Whose room
but yours, my dreaming brother? I see you now.

For you I bring my hand down through the fire.
It is for your sake that the flames rise through it.
What is it you are reaching out to hold,

to cling to, but your waking? Time to wake.
Time to embrace this, now your dreaming's over.
This is the nature now of all I am.

—In memory of Beth Shapiro (1946–1995)